THE GREATEST WELSH XV EVER

The Greatest
Welsh XV Ever

Eddie Butler

Published in 2011 by
Gomer Press, Llandysul, Ceredigion, SA44 4JL

ISBN 978 1 84851 408 9

A CIP record for this title is available from the British Library

© text: Eddie Butler, 2011
© photographs: Huw Evans, 2011 (unless otherwise acknowledged)

This book is published with the financial support of the
Welsh Books Council

The publishers would also like to acknowledge the generous contributions made
by the Huw Evans Picture Agency and Colorsport to the publication of this book.

www.colorsport.co.uk

Printed and bound in Wales at
Gomer Press, Llandysul, Ceredigion

CONTENTS

INTRODUCTION

An apology is no way to start a celebration of the best of Wales, but this has not been nearly as straightforward as I thought it would be. And I should like to say sorry to all those that have missed out, that have not received even a mention in the final draft, or that I have simply overlooked. I am sorry that I have let my bias show, but would argue that no team has ever been picked objectively. I apologise for drifting off the subject at times, but one thing always leads to another in Welsh rugby, and even in the most accomplished teams, not everything runs in a straight line. Sometimes we drift.

I wish I hadn't drawn so heavily on events whose archive is incomplete and that occurred when I was at my most impressionable. The Lions tours of 1971 and 1974 took place in an age before multi-camera live broadcasts in New Zealand and South Africa, and even the participants didn't seem particularly struck by – or even interested in – the magnitude of their achievements. But I think that says more about the mores of that time than any diminution of the tours' worth through lack of triumphalism. Perhaps modesty has its reward here.

Finally, I do not expect you to agree. Something would be strangely amiss and very un-Welsh if this selection won universal approval. But I do hope – and I don't think it's too wrong to set out with hope – that you will find some fun in your disagreement.

'JPR . . . the most evocative initials in sport.'
Full-back John Peter Rhys Williams about to clear
his lines for the '74 Lions in South Africa.

(Colorsport)

Chapter 1

15

FULL-BACK

To begin not at the beginning, but at the back. On the team sheet, in time-honoured style, the full-back comes first. This comes as a relief because elsewhere there have been so many question marks against so many positions and names that there has been a danger of indecision ruling and of these pages remaining blank. But here at 15 there is clarity, and this selection will have a grand opening. And yet, at the very moment of reaching for the keyboard and tapping out the three letters that remain to this day among the most evocative initials in sport, images of characters from different teams and other times began to flash and infiltrate. How can it be that there are rivals?

For speed over the ground there has been no finer sight than the 18-year-old Keith Jarrett in his first game for Wales, belting down the touchline so fast that not an English hand was laid upon him. It was

France's Serge Blanco, the antithesis of JPR.

a breathtaking performance in the final game of the Five Nations of 1967 by the full-back and not merely for that try. He also landed five conversions and two penalties for a tally of 19 points. It seemed that he was destined for greatness. Before long, however, he was more a centre than a full-back and not much further down the line he was a rugby league player, disappearing into semi-obscurity in Cumbria with Barrow. And not long after that he was lost to both codes of rugby, suffering a brain haemorrhage that brought his sporting career to an abrupt halt. He arrived as a teenager and retired at the age of 25.

Paul Thorburn might not enter the shortlist of contenders as a full-back who could split a line with effortless grace. Certainly he was no Serge Blanco, the Frenchman whose running made his team-mates in the 1980s and 1990s say that he left no traces in snow. But there in the mind's eye looms Thorburn's number 15 shirt, rising with his shoulders for one last intake of breath, steaming slightly, turned to the camera as he takes stock before beginning his run-up. Far away lie the posts, in Rotorua, and this is to be the conversion that will beat Australia and claim third place for Wales at the inaugural World Cup of 1987.

Paul Thorburn, prodigious goal kicker, gets tangled in the French defence.

In for Halfpenny, in for a pound.
Another fearless Welsh full-back,
Leigh Halfpenny, shone at the 2011 World Cup.

At the National Stadium in Cardiff a year earlier, the posts could have been called closer to home. But they were so ridiculously distant that when Thorburn indicated it was his intention to go for goal from a penalty awarded against Scotland, a strange noise came from the crowd: a rumble of disbelief, a chortle at the cheek of it. The distance was 70 yards 8½ inches (64.2 metres), the longest kick landed in international rugby. Paul Thorburn may not have been the most elegant runner, but he was the most prodigious kicker.

On the subject of full-backs who converted to rugby league, one of the most revered figures at Leeds RLFC is Lewis Jones. If he had stayed in union longer perhaps he would be challenging seriously for the full-back spot, but he went north after winning only nine caps for Wales and going on one Lions tour, as a replacement for George Norton, in 1950 to New Zealand and Australia. Lewis though cannot really be considered. Success as a Lion will obviously count in a candidate's favour, but staying power is part of the filtering process.

On those two scores there must be a place for Terry Davies. There has only ever been one victorious Lions tour to New Zealand, the

Shouldering responsibility. JPR clatters Gourdon into touch at the corner flag in the 1976 Grand Slam decider.
(Colorsport)

one inspired by Carwyn James in 1971. All Welshmen on that tour are going to come into the reckoning, since to beat the All Blacks in their own back yard remains perhaps the most formidable challenge in the game. New Zealanders can be cruelly dismissive of anyone who fails to cut the mustard, and have a particular disregard for the incoming tours of 1966, 1983 and 2005, but that is not to say that they are drawn only to winners. There remains respect and affection for the tourists of 1959, who lost the series 3–1, but who played some dazzling rugby, famously scoring four tries in the first Test in Dunedin, only to lose to six penalties by Don Clarke.

It is said that the crowd at the final Test at Eden Park in Auckland actively supported the Lions, who won 9–6, with four Welsh forwards in the pack – Ray Prosser, Rhys Williams, John Faull and Haydn Morgan – and Terry Davies at full-back. Now, while much of New Zealand's admiration was reserved for the elusive running on the wings of Tony O'Reilly and Peter Jackson, and the creative play of Bev Risman, Dave Hewitt and Ken Scotland, they also appreciated the defensive bravery of the single Welshman, Davies.

His refusal to budge was confirmed a year later, when he played for Llanelli against South Africa. The 1960 Springboks were, as the saying goes, uncompromising and their wing/centre François Roux was particularly ferocious, felling – late, early, on time – anyone who stood in his way. Terry Davies was that person at Stradey Park, but instead of backing away he put Roux, as another saying goes, on his arse.

But here we come back to the three initials that stand apart: JPR. The surname – Williams for the record – is an optional extra. For defiance, there has never been a player so uncompromisingly dismissive of his own welfare. Here was a doctor with a total disregard for personal safety. The tackle that clattered Jean-Francois Gourdon into touch in the corner in the Grand Slam decider of 1976 would by today's requirements to use the arms be quite illegal. On that day it was heroic. The speed with which he flew from full-back into the mayhem of the fighting on the 1974 Lions tour would by today's disciplinary procedures be reprehensible. At the time, his appetite for the fray warned the South Africans that they could win on no front.

It is tempting to say in the quest for an all-round view, that if he could catch and tackle with a technical precision to complement his lust for contact, he could not float like Blanco. He could not cut a line like John Gallagher or Christian Cullen of New Zealand, or beat

Decisive and incisive, New Zealand's Christian Cullen in Munster colours.

Australia's Kurtley Beale scores against Wales at the Millennium Stadium.

Fifteen to one.
Scotland's Andy Irvine
dares to enter JPR's domain.

(Colorsport)

a tackler with the laconic ease of the new sensation, Kurtley Beale of Australia. But JPR counter-attacked with a spirit bordering on the maniacal, and if he did not make tacklers regularly appear foolish he often enough left them in a heap. The rock under the high ball could be transformed in a flash into a mad pirate.

He was not a brilliant kicker. On the other hand, when it mattered most he put boot to ball from 45 metres and dropped the goal that squared the match that secured the Lions that one and only series win in New Zealand. The final Test in 1971 in Auckland: New Zealand 14 The Lions 14. Everybody on both sides rubbed their eyes. JPR raised his arms and wheeled away as if had been the most natural thing in the world. He couldn't in everyday conditions kick the ball half the distance of Lee Byrne, but it was as if he knew that he had one launch – and just the one – in his system and that he had better choose the moment of release with care. He had an instinct not just for the recklessly valiant but also a nose for the unexpected.

He wasn't perfect. In 1981, having retired from the international game at the end of the golden age of the 1970s, he attempted a comeback. In truth, he was not the player he once had been. Looking mortal did not become him. History, though, can be kind, shrinking that unfortunate period into a fleeting error of judgement, to be buried beneath the memories of what he was at his peak.

It is easier, therefore, to pick somebody from the past over a player still actively involved. Lee Byrne, for example, at the start of the Lions tour to South Africa in 2009, having starred in Wales's Grand Slam campaign of 2008, was surely on course to make Bridgend the home of two legendary full-backs, JPR having been born there, too. But Byrne was injured on tour and has not been at his best since. He had a trademark routine of kick, chase and regather, skills that set him apart from all others. But with a loss of confidence since injury, the signature three-part solo act has disappeared. History cannot yet say whether this is a pause or simply the end of the road for a player who could have been a contender. In his 30s, Byrne will have to do something extravagantly good at Clermont Auvergne to regain lost ground on the man even the French know automatically by his initials: JPR. The die is cast; the first name is down on the team sheet.

Lee Byrne, master of the kick, chase and regather.

A subtler moment for JPR.

'Blind terror took me to some very interesting places.'
Right wing Gerald Davies in full flight for London Welsh.

(Colorsport)

Chapter 2

14

RIGHT WING

The names in the frame for this position are already in the envelope. Three of them, and now it is simply a question of sorting them into an order of preference. Not that the final selection process promises to be easy, and before the end of this chapter the confession may have to be made that Ken Jones, Gerald Davies and Ieuan Evans were thrown into the air to see which way they landed.

Being tossed around was sometimes the reality of life for our contenders, even if their position was offered as a refuge for the slight, the graceful and the nippy. As rugby clung to the tenet that it was a game for all shapes and sizes, the wing was sacredly held as somewhere beyond the reach of those of less sensitive constitution, the beasts that would casually tear apart the limbs of the beautiful. Trying a long time ago to analyse the workings of the small in a sport dominated by the

Jonah Lomu of New Zealand: super-wing!

Towering and terrifying, Matt Banahan of England, the new breed of winger.

large, I once asked Gerald if his elusiveness was inspired by nothing more complicated than the fear of falling into the arms of his pursuers. 'Unquestionably,' he replied. 'Blind terror took me to some very interesting places.'

The theory was shattered by the arrival of the super-wing. Jonah Lomu of New Zealand in the mid-1990s had the most revolutionary impact on the role-reversal, the hunted turned carnivore, but it could be said that John Kirwan had paved the way – and clattered innumerable tacklers out of his path – a decade earlier. At the World Cup of 1987 Kirwan was the sensation of the tournament, and if Lomu scattered England players in the semi-final of 1995, it was his taming by the Springboks in the final that was the story of rugby's third World Cup.

Since then, the wings of the world have been growing ever more towering, up to and beyond the two-metre mark in the case of Matt Banahan of England. Maxime Medard of France has the lupine appearance and height of somebody more at home in the pack, a suitably feral partner for Sebastien Chabal, but he plays on the wing or at full-back. Even so, the right wing position still offers a place to those lacking a trig point on their crown, although health and safety dictate that he has to be wrapped in a protective layer of muscle nowadays. If Evans was halfway to being bulked up, Jones and Davies remained, at their biggest, merely wiry.

It matters not a jot. If they had been playing now they would all have done the necessary work in the gym to survive the onslaught of players whose livelihood depends on a tackle-count. There could be no guarantee of absolute safety, but they would have an extra layer of insulation and their chances of survival would depend now as they did then on pace and balance – and fear. Muscle may be the chosen fibre of the professional game, but speed and the fear of being dismembered are still the essential fabric of rugby on the wing.

I mention this correlation between size and fear and speed because I remember seeing Ieuan putting himself through a rehabilitation programme in 1995. In October 1994 his escape mechanisms had for once failed and he was left on the field looking at an ankle pointing the wrong way at the end of his leg. Tibia and fibula had been broken, and just about every ligament stretched beyond endurance, but here he was, a few months later, just before the game was thrown into professionalism, tied to tractor tyres, dragging them behind him,

'Merlin the Magician.'
Ieuan Evans in conjuring
mood against Ireland.

Teenage sensation George North cuts a swathe through the prostrate Fijian defence at the 2011 World Cup.

flogging himself in an attempt to regain his sharpness. Was he still in discomfort? 'Hurts like hell,' he said and carried on hauling his burden through the mud.

This was not a thoroughbred at work but a mule, bending its back to recapture the gift of speed. It was not, however, punishment without reward, because in 1997 he would go on his third Lions tour, the victorious adventure to South Africa. And in 1998 he would end his club career by winning the Heineken Cup with Bath against Brive in Bordeaux. Fear drives a wing away from danger; courage pulls him back into the thick of the action.

What else are we looking for in our right wings? On his side of the field there is perhaps more of a demand to chase kicks by a right-footed scrum-half than on the left. Ploughing a furrow up the touchline in pursuit of box-kicks, often with little prospect of laying a hand on the ball, is not what makes a fast runner volunteer to play on the wing. He dreams only of passes that put him into space, if only half a yard of freedom, in which he might strut his stuff.

He must be prepared to wait. Fewer good passes go left to right from players whose stronger guiding hand, usually the right, favours a delivery the other way. Patience, then, is a virtue, an obligation. In their day – and the three of them neatly cover every decade from 1950 to

2000 – there was a tendency to grow cold on bad days. The instruction to go looking for work had not definitively been given, and Ieuan might therefore argue that his burst into midfield for the try he scored for Llanelli against Australia in 1992, in a win to rival the Scarlets' victory two decades earlier over the New Zealand All Blacks, was ahead of its time. His celebration with his scrum-half, Rupert Moon, belly to belly, was not so groundbreaking.

No, on days when the forwards could not gain the upper hand, or when the weather was bad, or the passing poor, it was the lot of the right wing to shiver and wring his hands, and to put his head down and run yet again up the touchline rut without the ball, with nothing to look forward to but colliding with the catcher, the full-back who has dropped nothing all day . . .

But the wing chases because it is not always a lost cause. When back-row forward Emyr Lewis, of all people, stabbed a kick through against England, the first thought through Ieuan's mind might have been that an early pass to hand would have been the better option, because Rory Underwood and Jonathan Webb seemed to have the deeper situation well covered. But off the Wales wing dutifully ran, and suddenly there was a hesitation by England's wing, a flicker of doubt, a

Llanelli's Emyr Lewis passing, not kicking, this time.

'He's behind you! No, he's not: he's in front of you!'
Ieuan Evans passes Rory Underwood on his way to score against England at Cardiff in 1993.

Taking it all in his stride, Olympic sprinter and 1950 Lions wing, Ken Jones.

(South Wales Argus)

Grin or grimace? Gerald Davies crosses the line against Argentina.

momentary breakdown in communication between the defenders. It was all Ieuan needed, and England's lapse was converted into a Welsh try that led to their single victory in the Five Nations of 1993.

It was not quite the work of Merlin the Magician, the words used by BBC commentator Bill McLaren at the end of Evans's signature try against Scotland in 1988. If the other grand try of his career, against Australia in the final Test of the Lions tour of 1989, was a prosaic fall on the ball following an error of judgement by David Campese, whose creative bursts usually produced more positive results, this try against Scotland was a marvel. A series of sidesteps carried him from the touchline to the goal line near the posts, a trail of blue shirts sprawled behind him. Kicks must be chased, but this try is why wings play rugby.

Ken Jones on the field stretches back before even my time. He lives on most famously as a black and white blur, collecting a cross-kick by Clem Thomas (back-row forward kicking to right wing – there seems to be a theme here) in the last victory by Wales over the All Blacks, in 1953. There was nevertheless a lot more to him than this try: 44 caps for starters, a world record at the time for international appearances; 17 tries for the Lions on the 1950 tour to New Zealand; a silver medal in the 4 x 100 metre relay at the London Olympics of 1948; a long career in journalism when his days in rugby and athletics were over.

Gerald Davies was a centre moved to the wing by Clive Rowlands, the Wales coach who, as a player, probably tested the patience of more right wings with his box kicking than any scrum-half in the history of the game. The 111 line-outs in the game against Scotland in 1963 speak of a different strategy from the Evans game of 1988. The decision to shift Davies out to the wing was, however, visionary and the convert soon became one of the outstanding players in a team brimful with icons. He darted his way through the 1970s, never losing an inch of speed as he cut inside and outside. He won 46 caps for Wales and played in five Tests for the Lions, a total that would have grown had he not turned down the invitation to go to South Africa in 1974. In New Zealand in 1971 he scored three tries in the series won by the Lions.

Jones, Evans and Davies, like a Welsh firm of solicitors. If I have a special regard for the last of the partners it is only because I can say that I was there, flailing in his wake, on the day he touched the ball four times and scored four tries. It was for Cardiff in a cup game on Pontypool Park in 1978. Wings, please remember, do not score tries when their forwards do not win a fair share of ball, when the weather is

Gerald Davies frightening the life out of Bryan Williams with an early tackle during the second Test of the '71 Lions series in New Zealand.
(Colorsport)

bad and the going heavy. But Gerald skipped uphill on scraps through the mud to defeat us. We loved and hated him.

But I leave the final decision to Bryan Williams, the great All Black wing who was the Lomu of his day, a thunderous runner with thighs the girth of a grain silo. He had stormed through South Africa in 1970 and the next year, as a 20-year old, faced the Lions. 'Gerald Davies frightened the life out of me,' he told me in Auckland, on the day before he became president of the New Zealand Rugby Football Union in their 2011 World Cup year. 'I thought I was pretty quick, but to know this Welshman was about to come past me, or about to step and leave me in a spin, I can tell you, made a big impression on me.'

It is this role reversal – the little wing giving a giant of the game sleepless nights – that settles the issue. Gerald Davies comes down from the air first and goes in at number 14.

Gerald pauses for thought against Ireland in 1971.
(Colorsport)

RIGHT WING—14

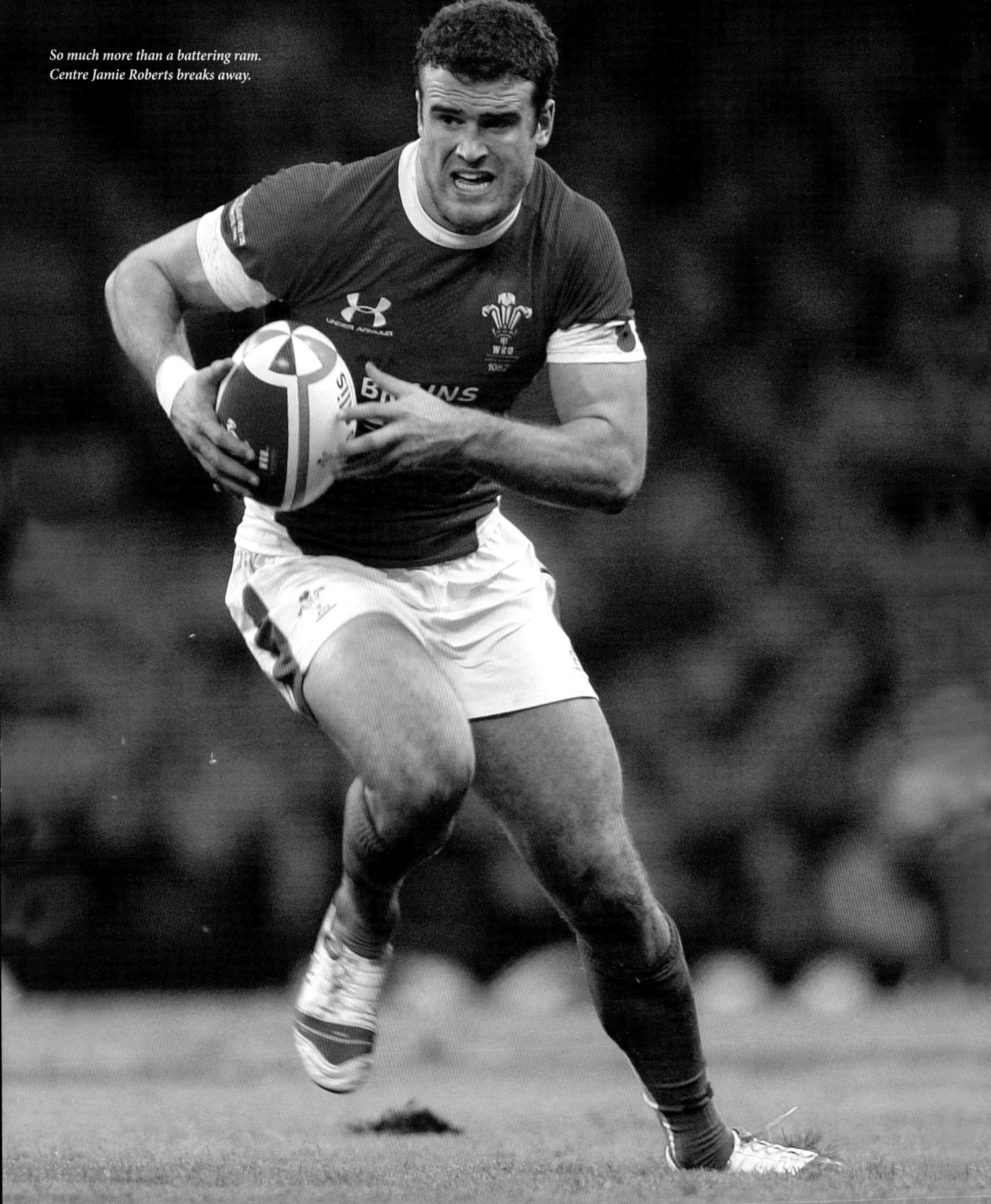

So much more than a battering ram.
Centre Jamie Roberts breaks away.

Chapter 3

13 & 12
THE CENTRES

Centres come in pairs, not only as a statement of the blindingly obvious, but also as historical double acts: Rhys Gabe and Gwyn Nicholls; Claude Davey and Wilf Wooller; Bleddyn Williams and Jack Matthews; Steve Fenwick and Ray Gravell. They are unlike the partnership inside them, the half-backs, because it would not be possible to ask a scrum-half like Rob Howley to play at 10, nor Jonathan Davies to feed the ball into the scrum, at least not to the liking of any hooker. There are specialists on the field and there are positions with a shared array of skills.

Both centres must pass, tackle, keep a defensive line in shape and generally manage the options before them. Is now the moment to pass, or is it to be contact first? I would have been tempted to sub-divide them into inside and outside, the job of the first to blast over the gain-

The pragmatic Steve Fenwick.

Ray Gravell in his own energised force-field.

line, and the second's to perfect the gliding arc that carries him on the outside of his marker, but John Dawes put me straight. When I asked the captain of the 1971 Lions whether he preferred inside or outside, left or right, 12 or 13, he simply said that Arthur Lewis and he picked up their shirts, 'as printed in the programme.'

He pointed out that even in his day, when structures were more rigidly observed on the field – because play rarely went beyond a third phase – there was an encouragement to take up a position according to instinct once everyone had been moved around a bit. I think he was referring more to himself here, since his partner, Lewis, was more likely to stick close to his starting position and run ramrod-straight whatever the situation. But if Dawes was sliding up the blind side, taking a pass directly from Gareth Edwards at scrum-half, the number 12 or 13 ceased to be relevant.

So, if numbers are interchangeable, do we go for a contemporaneous pairing or for two individuals from different era? There is something romantic about the centre partnership. Gabe and Nicholls were of a seemingly carefree Edwardian age, when Wales alone could beat the All Blacks, as they did in 1905. Davey and Wooller formed an outsized pairing for their day, but one was the captain and the other the inspiration when Wales beat the All Blacks in 1935. Williams and Matthews remained locked together – always turned out nattily over a pint in the Cardiff Athletic Club or up at the Butcher's Arms in Llandaff, looking at the modern game fondly, never sourly – way beyond their time on the field with Cardiff, Wales and the Lions of 1950. Bleddyn and Doctor Jack: the one so elegant and graceful that he was known as the 'Prince of Centres', the other so hard that the only benefit to tangling with him was that he could immediately administer medical aid to the parts he had damaged with his tackling.

Fenwick and Gravell formed the centre pairing in the second half of the golden age of the 1970s, and into the more troubled 1980s. Fenwick was the more pragmatic, never given to overestimating his groundspeed, but contrastingly speedy of thought and armed with a cannon of a right boot. 'Grav', on the other hand, could not have been less suited for a world where common sense sometimes had to prevail. He lived in an energised force-field of devotion to his homeland and only infrequently emerged from the depths of its wonderful and weird red mist.

*Size, speed and skill,
Jamie Roberts lets Fiji see it
all at the 2011 World Cup.*

'An icon in his own right.'
Scott Gibbs splits the English
defence at Wembley in 1999.

I remember whiling away a Sunday afternoon with Grav in a sleepy, low-ceilinged bar in Paris. He was telling the barman what it was like to play against the mighty French teams of the 1970s and how Jo Maso, curly and deft opposite him, offered a challenge so very different from that of Alain Estève and Michel Palmié, forwards whose clutches were best avoided. He began to describe the dangers of falling into the embrace of the giant second rows and because his French was limited he resorted to universal sign language. Unfortunately, Grav's re-enactment of one particular brawl on the Parc des Princes sent his arms into the air, and down came the tiles of the low ceiling on his head. 'Wild men, those French,' he said through a cloud of dust.

But if we choose ready-made pairs, what about all those individual Welsh centres that have shone, or struck up partnerships with players from other countries? Scott Gibbs was an icon in his own right for Wales, his try against England in 1999 at Wembley the rugby highlight that ushered out the twentieth century. And yet he was even more effective on Lions tours, teaming up with Jeremy Guscott in New Zealand in 1993 and in South Africa in 1997. He scored with a typical burst of power in the final Test at Eden Park in Auckland against the All Blacks to give the tourists brief hope of taking the series. New Zealand responded to win 30–13 and perhaps the series is remembered not so much for the solitary try by the Lions but as evidence of how the All Blacks respond when threatened with defeat at home.

On the next tour the Lions had the series won before the final Test and their defining image was the squat Gibbs sending the giant Springbok prop, Os du Randt, sprawling. For all that grace and elusiveness define the Welsh way of playing rugby, sometimes you can't beat a reminder that it remains a game of physical contact. 'Of physical combat,' according to Lucien Mias, the great captain of the first French team to win the Five Nations title, in 1959, and who, incidentally, later swapped life as a teacher for medicine. He became a doctor specialising in Alzheimer's in the town where he played his rugby, Mazamet.

Gibbs was combative in the extreme, but he prospered in the company of the more flowing Guscott, just as Jamie Roberts flowered alongside Brian O'Driscoll and expanded his repertoire in South Africa a dozen years after the 1997 tour. He had made a mark as a line-battering 12, the fearless search for contact never more evident than in his alarming clash of heads with Stirling Mortlock in 2008. The Australian captain departed immediately, while Roberts played on for

Gibbs's flowing Lions partner, Jeremy Guscott of England.

Best of mates!
Ireland's Brian O'Driscoll forgets old allegiances as he embraces Jamie Roberts.

a few minutes, even playing a part in Wales's first try. Eventually the medical student had to follow some diagnostic guidelines. 'My head was squeaking. I guessed there was something wrong.'

Such collisions in the centre are more frequent than they used to be, even if the midfields of today have been crowbarred apart at the scrummage by the five-metre law that places the three-quarters that distance from the rearmost foot of the set piece. In general, however, the three-quarters have advanced as two lines until they now stand – although most of the time they are going at full tilt – in whispering distance of each other. Passes break the speed of sound to avoid interception. There is less subtlety because there is more contact. Forwards, by way of contrast, have been ordered apart. At the line-out, for example, where once they jostled in a maze of intertwining obstruction they must respect the gap. Front rows must observe the lengthy ritual of 'Crouch, touch, pause, engage,' an incantation that grows ever more prolonged. This is scrummaging by Gregorian chant, and just goes to show that separation is the name of the new game, everywhere bar the centre.

When Jamie Roberts went on the Lions tour in the summer of 2009 there were few predictions that he was on the verge of broadening his angle of vision in this world built for size and forthrightness. And yet, in the company of O'Driscoll, he was suddenly so much more than a battering ram. He was to be seen cutting angles, interchanging passes long and short with his partner. Above all, he honed the timing of his run so that he accelerated into the tackle. This was twin-speed centre play, and although the Lions of 2009 lost the series, the outcome could well have been different if Roberts and O'Driscoll had not been injured in the same extended passage of play in the second Test at Loftus Versfeld, Pretoria.

That is the most dramatic Test I have ever seen, influenced hugely by the centres on both sides, but in particular by Roberts and O'Driscoll. While they were on the field, they held sway. When O'Driscoll was concussed, Bryan Habana ran through into a gap the Irishman would in his right mind have filled. With both centres gone, Jaque Fourie barged over for a late try. The swing of the game was also influenced by the rise and then the departure of two Welsh props, who will have their say in later sections. By some strange coincidence, they too were injured simultaneously and had to depart. It was a Test won not on the feats of those that arrived, but lost at the point of departure

'The fearless search for contact.'
Jamie Roberts takes on South
Africa at the 2011 World Cup.

Tom Shanklin (above) and Gavin Henson, Grand-Slam-winning centre combination in 2005.

'A sense of partnership.'
Jonathan Davies and Jamie Roberts.

of two pairs. A match of medically unsound intensity went the way of the Springboks, 28–25, but the point remains that Roberts and O'Driscoll, when sound of limb and clear of thought, cut to shreds the defence that day, as they did any defence they faced, despite being the most marked combination in the game. At the end of the tour, Roberts was named man of the series.

He then entered a phase of stasis. I have a theory that at home he is half rugby pro and half medical student, and only on tour or at the World Cup does be become a full-time giant. He returned from South Africa and could not do for Wales what he had done for the Lions. Perhaps it was ongoing problems with injury, or the more conservative style adopted by Wales in the build-up to the 2011 World Cup, or perhaps none of the centres placed alongside him, from Gavin Henson to Tom Shanklin, Andrew Bishop and James Hook could work out the equations of time and space quite like O'Driscoll. Only with the arrival of the youngsters, Jonathan Davies – the version of the 21st century – and Scott Williams was there a sense of partnership in the midfield.

Or perhaps it was all about the supply chain from the player inside him. In New Zealand at the World Cup, Jamie Roberts suddenly found his deliverer, the outside half with the slightly worried face of a doubter, but with the silky skills of a passer who knew exactly what he was doing. Rhys Priestland, in the space of just a few weeks, went from being the understudy to Stephen Jones and James Hook to the most creative distributor in the world game. Priestland was the player who put Jamie Roberts back into space. And how the centre responded, erupting against South Africa and sounding the blast, heard from one tip of New Zealand to the other, that Wales were about to become the sensation of the tournament. Even in defeat to France, when Wales were without the injured Priestland and down to fourteen with the dismissal of Sam Warburton, Roberts was never anything less than sensational.

His assault on the advantage line certainly places him in a different bracket of inside centre from Mike Gibson. The Irishman was an outside half who went on to play centre, a precursor to a trend that was successfully adopted in Wales, with Mark Ring, Bleddyn Bowen, David Richards. They all brought poise on the ball to the position, but none could ever be a second Gibson. He filled the record books of Irish rugby in his international career of 69 caps and five Lions tours over 15 years. He was quite simply the complete footballer, never off balance, tough beyond what seemed possible from a physique less Himalayan than Roberts's, and razor-sharp of mind. His partnership with John Dawes in 1971 was particularly effective. The more Colin Meads swore at you the more you knew the mighty All Black second row and captain appreciated in his heart of hearts your play. And Meads abused Gibson roundly – not as much as he did one other particular player, and to that berated Welshman we shall come later . . .

No, Gibson impressed New Zealand no end, but there was also respect for Dawes. The All Blacks acknowledged that they were well beaten on the coaching front, where Carwyn James was always several steps ahead of Ivan Vodanovich, and on the front of what we might call, a bit boringly, general management. This included the preparations before kick-off and the on-field decisions that a captain must make. Somehow the influence of Dawes has dwindled outside New Zealand down the years, perhaps because the unseen guidance of the captain is not as interesting as JPR's drop goal or Gerald Davies's sidestep.

Dawes brought thoughtfulness to the 12 position. If Jamie Roberts was not blessed with a quick pair of hands, perhaps the captain of 1971 might shade it. But there was more to Roberts at the World Cup than bludgeoning forthrightness. He swept the ball across his chest in a flash to release George North and defended with a courage that won the hearts and admiration of New Zealand. Jamie Roberts, take the shirt.

What complimentary skills might be required at 13 then? Somebody armed with the hand-off of John Devereux or James Hook, the physical intensity of Gravell or Mike Hall or Mark Taylor? Or do we look for a little more guile, the grace of Allan Bateman, the little steps and passes of Leigh Davies, the intelligence of Nigel Davies – a sort of Conrad Smith of his day – or the daring of Malcolm Price, who scored two tries in the famous defeat to New Zealand in Dunedin in 1959: Don Clarke 18 (6 penalties) The Lions 17 (4 tries)? Perhaps a centre with a dummy? I appreciate that nobody at international level should ever buy one, but do you remember the day in 1984 when the entire island of Ireland tilted before the feinted pass of Robert Ackerman, and tilted back at his second?

The dummy is an echo of more forgiving times, when artistry was allowed to reveal itself in space. With the shrinkage of the second, there is less room for the first. Instead we have Ma'a Nonu. But at the risk of bowing slightly before the oncoming freight train, I'm going for beauty before the bosh, and selecting Bleddyn Williams. There is

John Dawes leads out the Barbarians against the All Blacks in that 1973 game.

New Zealand's World-Cup-winning centres Conrad Smith and Ma'a Nonu have Matthew Rees in their sandwich.

Jamie Roberts defies New Zealand's Jerome Kaino's tackle to score at the Waikato Stadium in 2010.

not much footage of the Prince of Centres at work – and his career included leading both Cardiff and Wales to victory over the All Blacks in 1953, all in the space of two weeks – but he goes in because of the way people who do remember him talk about him. And it's not what they say, but how they say it, reducing their volume to stress their reverence. Bleddyn Williams electrified a generation of onlookers and fellow players and hushed their tones whenever they spoke of him thereafter. Old film reveals him to have been an upright runner, a bit in the mould of Cliff Morgan, without the head thrown so far back. The only indication of his class from these brief glimpses from 60 years ago is the trail of defenders, failed tacklers who had dived and missed, and this lone runner somehow leaving them all behind.

He didn't play for Wales until 1947, when he was still just 23, but there is no doubt that he would have been capped earlier were it not for the second world war. Having trained as an RAF fighter pilot he found himself – 'I was volunteered,' he would say – flying gliders over the Rhine during the Allies' advance into Germany. He did beat one hasty retreat from the front line, being ordered by his commanding officer to explain what the devil he thought he was doing so far forward when he should be reporting for duty at Welford Road, where Great Britain the next day were to face the Dominions. He made it in time, and I believe I heard somebody mention that he scored the winning try. And fear not about his defence. It may have lacked the bone–jarring impact of Jack Matthews's tackles, but it is said – no, it is whispered reverentially – that nobody ever went round or through Bleddyn Williams.

Bleddyn Williams, always spoken of in reverential tones.

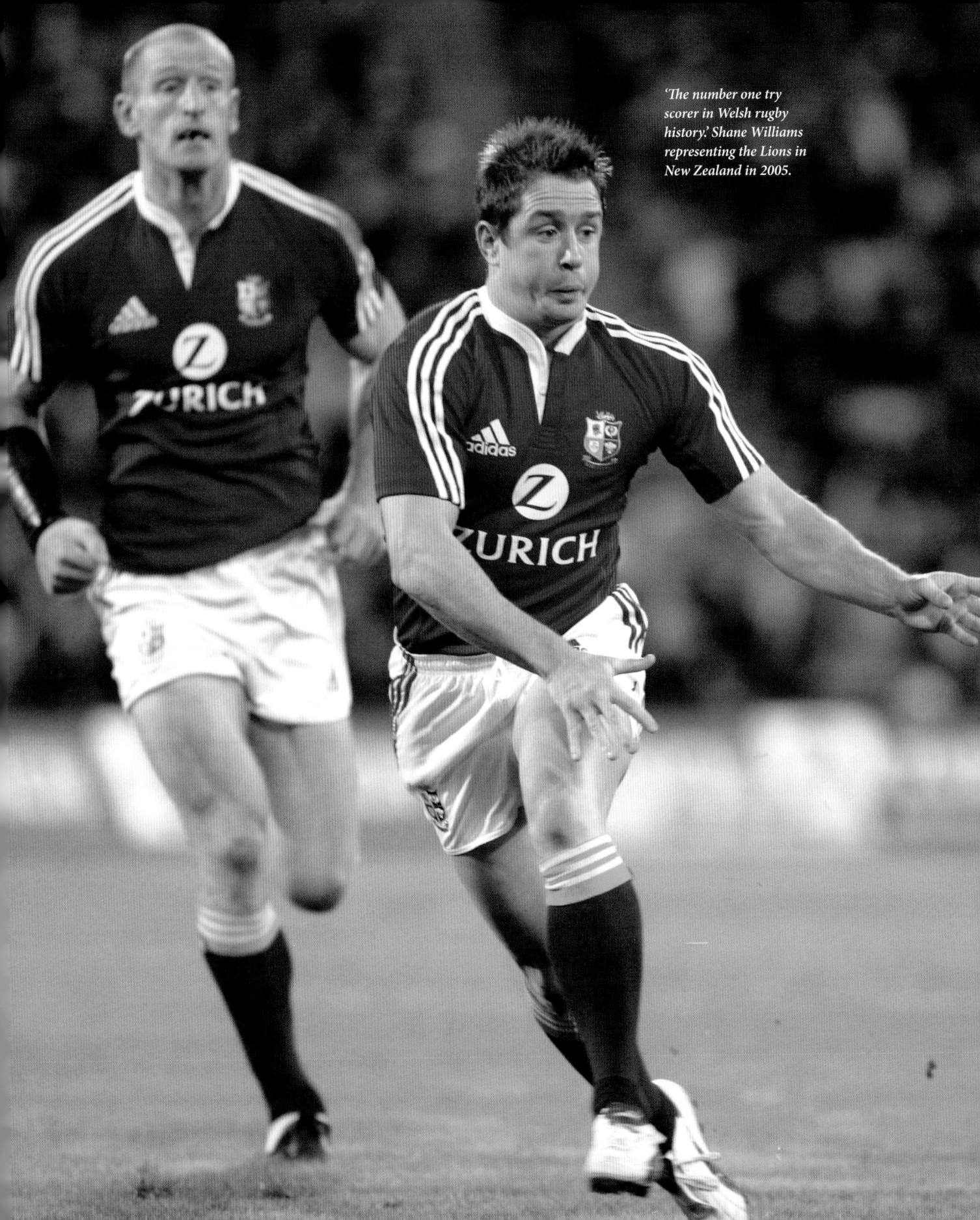

'The number one try scorer in Welsh rugby history.' Shane Williams representing the Lions in New Zealand in 2005.

Chapter 4

11

LEFT WING

It is at this point, as we reach the end of the three-quarter line and before we head for the half-backs and forwards, that I am conscious of an omission. Is there to be no mention of the first player to win 100 caps for Wales, who scored 40 tries over 12 years in international matches, a scoring tally that took him past Ieuan Evans as the leading try-scorer for his country? Is there to be no place for Gareth Thomas? Alfie, where are you?

No player in the history of Welsh rugby, with the possible exception of Arthur 'Monkey' Gould, has generated more headlines. Come to think of it, is there to be no mention of Gould? Yes, there is. Like Thomas, he was a versatile player, at home in the centre or at full-back? He was the undoubted first superstar of Welsh rugby, adored in his home town of Newport and beyond. He was the most capped centre,

with 25 appearances there (plus two at full-back) between 1885 and 1897, until Steve Fenwick in 1980. He led Wales more often than anyone, on 18 occasions, again a record that stood for nearly 100 years, until Ieuan Evans overtook him in 1994. I like the story of him standing around arguing with Billy Bancroft, a gifted full-back for Wales between 1890 and 1901 (his brother Jack played in the same position after him until 1919), about what to do with a penalty during the game against England. Captain Gould called for a place kick; Bancroft a drop-goal. Gould stamped his foot and threw the ball down in disgust, Bancroft picked it and dropped the goal that won the game and gave Wales their first Grand Slam.

In 1896 Gould was granted a public testimonial, and the fund, a shilling at a time, quickly grew to several hundreds of pounds. This brought Wales into conflict with rugby's laws of the time on amateurism. This was only a year after the breakaway by the northern clubs of England, to form what would become professional rugby league. Wales, not wanting to lose the chance to play against England, had, by and large, stayed within the supposedly unpaid code, but their definition of amateurism was a lot more flexible than their neighbour's.

Faced with expulsion, the Welsh Rugby Union at first yielded, but at a dinner in Gould's honour that same year he was given a house. Now that's some whip-round. The amateur establishment again expressed its stern disapproval. The Welsh public gave vent to equally strong feelings about where England might shove their self-righteousness, and the Welsh Rugby Union gave way this time to domestic pressure and withdrew their membership of the International Rugby Football Board. Wales played no international matches for a year, until in February 1898, inevitably, they re-entered the fold, vowing to observe and honour the regulations governing amateurism. Arthur Gould, admittedly by then 33, was not allowed to play again.

Gareth Thomas, first capped in 1995, the great year of revolution when rugby went 'open,' never needed to worry about payment. Like Gould, he would play for a dozen years and cover many positions, up and down the three-quarters. If this team were based on the number of corner-flagging, last-ditch, heroic tackles made, Thomas would be 11 or 12 or 13 or 14, but perhaps not 15, where JPR was even more maniacal. Alfie nevertheless was a monster, tall as a second row, chiselled to perfection and always deeply committed, in an age when Wales's rugby was not always bountiful. True, he was captain of the

Chiselled and deeply committed, Gareth Thomas leading the 2005 Lions in New Zealand.

Grand Slam side of 2005, but he missed half of the campaign, breaking his thumb against France. He was captain not only of his country, but also of the Lions, a stand-in for Brian O'Driscoll, who was infamously drilled into the Christchurch turf like a probe for oil, on the ill-fated tour to New Zealand in 2005.

But, my, how Alfie fell out with people. Coaches especially. He was dropped by Steve Hansen before the World Cup in 2003, led a revolt against Mike Ruddock after the Grand Slam of 2005, rubbished Gareth Jenkins in the World Cup of 2007 and was finally dumped by Warren Gatland, who wrote his telephone number on a blackboard and told the rest of the Welsh squad that their erstwhile skipper was from that moment on persona non grata.

And then there was his mini-stroke in the middle of this tumultuous time, in 2006. Alfie invited himself to appear one Sunday

Warren Gatland, another of Alfie's coaches.

Gareth Thomas celebrates victory over England in 2005 with Gavin Henson.

evening on *Scrum V,* the rugby programme on BBC Wales television. The phrase 'player power' was still written clearly in the dust of the fall-out from Mike Ruddock's resignation, and the captain wanted to have his say. 'You lot had better watch out,' warned the Wales manager, Alan Phillips, 'Alfie's gunning for you.' That included me, alongside Jonathan Davies in the studio.

What Alfie actually said on the matter of mutiny – as far as I can recall it was something to do with marching into the office of Steve Lewis, then the chief executive officer of the WRU, and only threatening strike action as a last resort, because medical insurance wasn't in place to cover treatment to the shoulder of the scrum-half, Gareth Cooper – has long been buried beneath what happened next. Alfie went home, started to watch the transmission of the recorded show and collapsed. And even this apparently serious medical condition – you don't mess with arteries in the neck – was soon forgotten, partly because he resumed playing soon enough, but mostly because he then announced he was gay. 'We know, Alfie,' said Welsh rugby. 'No, no, I'm gay,' he repeated. 'We know,' repeated everyone.

Alfie was – is – a natural star of the melodrama that is Welsh rugby, brilliant as a character in a changing room that was struggling and almost impossible in a changing room that was doing well. He was a tormented soul before he came out, and I think this made him a little restless, shall we say, when it came to taking a lead in the slightly overemotional life of the Welsh rugby camp. He was a supreme multi-positional player, his caps and his tries stating his case far more eloquently than anything he tended to say in rage at the more tortured moments of his despair. But on the matter of selection for the team of these pages, it is his status as an all-rounder that keeps him out. Alfie, where are you? On the bench, and go easy on the coach, please.

Rarely has so much space been devoted to a non-selection, but in a way the contenders for the left wing – I was going to say the true contenders, but that would be harsh – almost speak for themselves. They can be compressed into an ascending order, starting in third place with the youngster who went on the Lions tour of 1971 as a 20-year old and began to rampage his way around New Zealand, threatening every try-scoring record in the book.

John Bevan had won his first cap for Wales that same year in a Grand Slam campaign that ensured that the Lions would be strongly Welsh in flavour. This was not necessarily considered a strong point,

John Bevan in pursuit of the French at Cardiff in 1972.
(Colorsport)

at least not outside Wales. New Zealand had seen Wales on tour in 1969 and viewed them as prone to pangs of homesickness. The establishment of rugby union at home viewed Wales with general suspicion at the best of times – that fellow Gould had shown that the Welsh were never entirely to be trusted – and here were the Lions with a Welsh coach, Carwyn James, a Welsh captain, John Dawes, and a whole parade of barely domesticated Welsh players. Bevan? Hardly heard of the chap.

The relatively unknown wing from Cardiff, originally from Tylorstown in the Rhondda, soon put paid to the tag of unknown quantity. He scored six tries in his opening three games in New Zealand. In the first game that really made the Kiwis sit up and take notice of the Lions, the thumping victory over Wellington three weeks before the first Test, he scored four tries. He battered his way into the Test team for Carisbrook and the tourists won 9–3. At this point, it is true, he lost it a bit, and, yes, began to miss home. David Duckham replaced him for the final three Tests, but Bevan still ended up equalling the try-scoring record, set by Tony O'Reilly in 1959, of 17 tries in New Zealand. And he would score again in another victory over New Zealand, in the Barbarians game of 1973, before signing for Warrington in rugby league. He wasn't half bad at that, either.

Second place is going to hurt, because J.J. Williams on the Lions tour of 1974 was absolutely brilliant. The grounds were hard and the supply of ball coming his way from a pack of forwards that pulverised the Springboks by all means fair and foul meant that he had plenty of opportunities to show off the pace that had taken him to the Commonwealth Games as a sprinter in 1970. But there was much more to JJ than mere speed. If Gerald Davies on the right wing never seemed to lose a fraction of speed while sidestepping, so JJ could put the ball on his right boot and chip it ahead without breaking stride. And it wasn't a question of hit and hope, but a delicate placing of the ball into a vulnerable space for defenders. The kicking game is generally considered the dullard of a partner to the handling game, but JJ put it in a Ferrari.

Shane Williams, however, is handed the number 11 shirt. Why the 'however'? Well, I suppose it's because he never won with the Lions, only going on the terrible tour of New Zealand in 2005 and playing in the last Test of 2009, when South Africa already had the series won. On the other hand, in that last game, at Ellis Park, Johannesburg, he scored

J.J. Williams takes the field against Australia in 1975.   (Colorsport)

Shane Williams, under starter's orders.

Shane Williams dives over for his impossible try against Scotland at Cardiff in 2008.

A sweet moment for Shane, as he escapes the attentions of South African flyer, Bryan Habana.

two tries, taking awkward passes with ridiculous ease, and was named man of the match.

Perhaps it is the very fact of having had to battle permanently against the odds that makes his story so engaging. He was dismissed time and time again as too small to play at the top level, but always fought his way back into contention. He only went to the 2003 World Cup as a reserve scrum-half, but ended up as one of the stars of the tournament. Of course, he had to bulk up, but it became a point of honour as well as muscle to show his coaches that he was no more liable to lose the ball in contact than the next wing. He developed the wriggle of a terrier to be able to take the ball to ground on his terms.

But, hell, we don't love Shane because he can wriggle in contact; we love him because he can wriggle out of contact. We love his appetite for the ball, his elusiveness in tight spaces, the speed, the audacity that make him the number one try-scorer in Welsh rugby history by a country mile: the half-century mark was passed long ago, with Alfie way back in second on 40. Tommy Bowe of the Ospreys and Ireland, a wing/centre who is good enough in his own right to have been named player of the Six Nations in 2010, told me that he sometimes had to stop and shake his head in awe at what Shane could do with the ball, with his feet. It is worth mentioning that Shane also happens to be the best passer of the ball in the Welsh team, the best at straightening a line and the best reader of any given situation.

I have a favourite try, the one that was really not a try at all. It was against Scotland in 2008 and the connection between eye and mind and legs on his approach to the line was remarkable. There were defenders coming at him from the side, from behind and standing in front of him, but his brain worked out a way past them all. He had to change hands on the ball, he had to dive and stay out of touch. True, he didn't quite manage to avoid trailing a toe against the sideline, but the television match official, Carlo Damasco, was so caught up in the spirit of the moment that he decided it was a try.

One however simply leads to another, to the try for example that he scored in Pretoria against South Africa in the second Test of the difficult tour there in the summer of 2008. The ball came to him messily, bobbling along the floor from a scrappy breakdown and a rebound. This meant nobody had done any preparation work for him. He scooped up the ball and immediately beat a front-row forward on the outside, which was not the most demanding deed of his career,

Shane Williams, with Colin Charvis in support, makes the world sit up and take notice at the World Cup in 2003.

but it did allow him time to assess what lay ahead. Five more to beat, he would have told himself, just the full handful then, covering all the angles and lying in tiers before him. He cut in, away from the touchline, and then, instead of going in again, he veered back to the outside, down a narrow corridor between the touchline and these tacklers. They had checked slightly at his first sidestep infield and now they could not catch him. A single red shirt lay in a gang of green, with the referee's arm up for the try.

It is also true that sometimes we have had to shake our heads in frustration. We groan when he kicks the ball – he's no JJ – but he has won just about all of us over. The nation wants to sweep a protective wing around our Shane. We worry for his safety when he falls into the dark embrace of those that would hurt him. We love him for looking so worried, even if we know that beneath the creases there is a little warrior not unafraid to get stuck in. He looks like an angel, sometimes a cherub with a mullet or shaven-headed, but is a little scrapper, in or out of kit, and we love that too. To have had dust-ups the length and breadth of the Amman valley seals his place in our hearts and his selection on the left wing.

─── 11 ───

─────LEFT WING─────

*'Drop your shoulder and go!'
Shane demonstrates his sidestep to the
Australian defence at Cardiff in 2010,
as Mike Phillips stares in disbelief.*

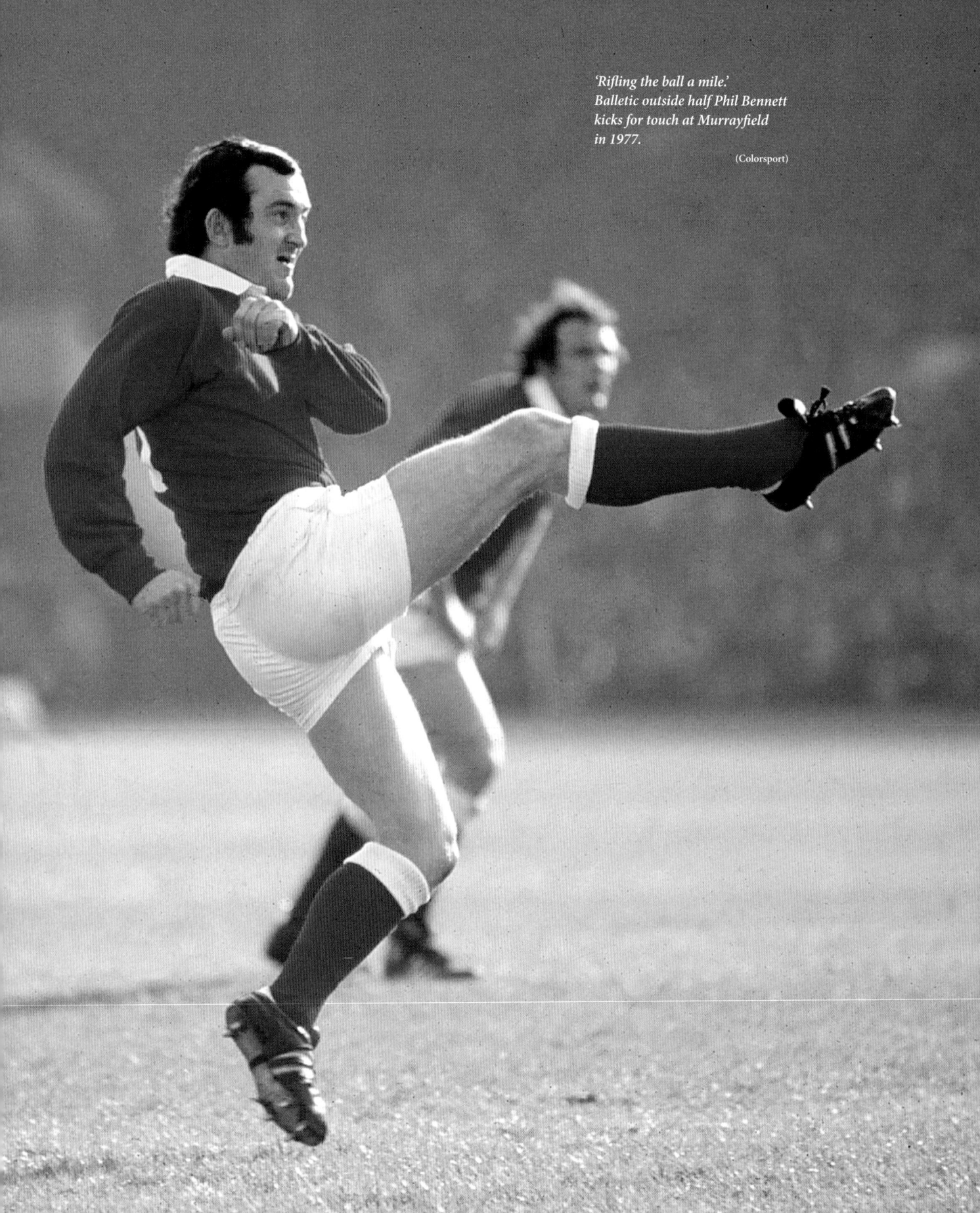

'Rifling the ball a mile.'
Balletic outside half Phil Bennett
kicks for touch at Murrayfield
in 1977.

(Colorsport)

Chapter 5

10

OUTSIDE HALF

This is the easiest position and the hardest. People seem to have a favourite, often determined by what they have seen with their own eyes, or has been passed down by word of mouth in the family, and they stick by their selection no matter what happens, no matter who appears on the scene. It is the Welsh position, it is our special shirt, he is the chosen one, and it is only right and proper that views are strongly held and staunchly defended. When it comes to the pub discussion about the best 10, the only unanimity comes at the end, when everybody agrees to differ.

It is the easiest because you could simply take a pin, wave it blindly and make a perfectly logical case for the name on which it lands. It is difficult because the list of names goes on and on. Perhaps we should treat our cherished outside half with the respect due to the democratic

Neil Jenkins

Cliff Morgan

David Watkins

process and change these particular pages into a voting slip. Put a cross against one name. No AV; first past the post wins.

On the other hand, I feel the flush of the tyrant's power. I can make a choice here without your help. In fact, all you've done is confuse the issue. So, let's make it personal. I can safely say that in all the time I was playing I had no interest in the history of rugby. That's not to say I don't go back a bit, because what now seems crusty was my present. Rugby began for me with Keith Jarrett against England in 1967, when I was nine. That would make David Watkins my starting point, and first impressions are always important.

That would at least narrow the field to the last five decades, but the more my present has become elongated, filling the eras of Barry John, Phil Bennett, Jonathan Davies, Neil Jenkins and Stephen Jones, the more inclined I have grown to go the other way, back in time. I have found myself drawn to the exploits of Percy Bush in 1905, the duel in the 1930 between Cliff Jones and Willie Davies, both schoolboy prodigies. And then you hit Cliff Morgan, positively worshipped in South Africa as 'Morgan the Magnificent' for his performances there with the Lions in the drawn series of 1955.

Famous names, ancient and modern, start to stockpile. What is more, there are plenty of not-so-celebrated players to salute, from Gareth Davies, Malcolm Dacey and Bleddyn Bowen to current players like James Hook and even the great enigma, Gavin Henson, 10s that we like to think would walk into many other countries' teams. I began to read about Billy Cleaver and I was willing him to be no good, but it was in vain, and I leave him out only because on the Lions tour of 1950 he played in three Tests as a full-back. It's time to be brutal, as we say in the business of being a tyrant.

The shortlist is: Barry John, Phil Bennett and Jonathan Davies. This is hard on the ghosts of the past who have been calling to me, but this is no time to be spooked. It is also hard on that first player to make an impression, David Watkins, who won six Lions caps in Australia and New Zealand in 1966, leading the Test side in Wellington and Auckland in the place of the official tour captain, Mike Campbell-Lamerton. If the 1966 Lions could not beat New Zealand, his club side could, Newport famously beating the All Blacks 3–0 in 1963. He went north to league in 1967 and the factor of not living a life in union to the full must count against him, even if he became as good at Salford and with Great Britain, if not better, as he had been at home.

James Hook, the latest in a long Welsh line of utility outside halves.

Jonathan Davies, spots a gap ahead.

Stephen Jones takes on New Zealand's Dan Carter in the 2005 Lions series.

Jonathan Davies went north, too. The pub row is starting to brew. And he never went on a Lions tour. It's true, but the first World Cup of 1987 took the place of a tour and there was nothing wrong with his form in that inaugural tournament, where Wales took third place. His form was even better when they went back to New Zealand the following year. Lucky them. They went on tour as Triple Crown champions, their outside half having been sensational in the 1988 Five Nations, only to run slap into one of the formidable sides of all time. The All Blacks included Sean Fitzpatrick, then a young hooker who had kept the captain, Andy Dalton, out of the World Cup side. It had Wayne 'Buck' Shelford at number 8, alongside Michael Jones, the greatest wing forward I have ever seen – and that includes Richie McCaw. If you managed to avoid those forwards then you had John Kirwan storming at you on the wing, or John Gallagher cutting through from full-back. Wales had played this All Blacks team in the semi-final of that first World Cup and had been hammered. Now they were thumped again, twice. But Jiffy was heroic and scored a try down the length of the field when others might have thumped the ball in misery out of the ground.

He wasn't quite so good in November 1988, his last game before going north to Widnes, but in my book anyone who suffers the ordeal of leading Wales to defeat at the hands of Romania deserves a break. Not even a tyrant can rewrite the history of Wales in Romania in 1983. Been there, done that. There are better experiences in a rugby life.

Shared woe aside, there is another reason for shortlisting Jonathan. The professionalisation of the game changed the outside half's role like no other. For Neil Jenkins and Stephen Jones, just about every square inch of the freedom afforded to Barry John and Phil Bennett in the 1960s and 1970s disappeared. And even worse than having less space in which to dance and slide and throw light on the company logo of the Welsh outside-half factory, there are now heavyweights running at full pelt into the very channel once reserved for artistes. In short, the modern outside half has to tackle.

Jonathan was not a good technical tackler, but he was a nasty tackler. He always had an elbow raised in what might charitably be called a position of self-defence. In reality it poked out as an offensive weapon. I make no criticism, for every small player in a big man's world has the right to raise arms. And Jonathan was the master of dishing out more pain than he ever received, satisfying the first law in the book of survival.

If you don't tackle you run the risk of being sold into rugby exile, like Danny Cipriani to the Melbourne Rebels. If you do tackle you run the risk of injury or of lying so deep that you strip all spontaneity from your performance. You become Jonny Wilkinson, a saint, a warrior that wouldn't lie down, but hardly a fly half to send a shiver down the spine. There's only one that does that nowadays and his name is Dan Carter, the single problem being that he is a New Zealander behind an All Black pack and with Sonny Bill Williams and Conrad Smith outside him. That does create a certain tingle.

Still, Carter is no more than Barry with a bit of bulk. The pub must be prepared to make allowances. Get Phil on the supplements and the weights, and he'd have been just like that Dan the Man. It's all true; we must accept that Barry and Phil would have taken a deep breath and started shifting the iron. It simply wasn't an obligation in their day.

They go head to head for the shirt because of their record: they won Grand Slams and they won on Lions tours. It's hard luck on the others but that's the way it is. Barry won in New Zealand in 1971 and Phil in South Africa in 1974. Both could leave the most snarling defenders laid out in their wake, the spittle of the aggressor now the dribbling of the humiliated. Barry was a glider; Phil a jagged sidestepper. Both kicked beautifully from hand, slender legs rifling the ball a mile.

Both lost on Lions tours: Barry in 1968 in South Africa, before he became King John in New Zealand three years later; Phil in New Zealand in 1977, three years after barely leaving an imprint of the dry surfaces of South Africa in '74. Is that to be the deciding margin, how they lost? Behind a Lions pack so dominant in '77 that the All Blacks opted to pack down in one scrummage with no more than a front row – three could go backwards no faster than the full eight had gone – Phil was expected to run the show. He didn't because it rained and rained. In 1971 the grounds were damp but the sun shone. In '77 there was water everywhere and Phil slid and slithered into trouble . . .

Is it to be Barry then? King John, who came home in 1971, played on for one more international campaign – Wales were denied the chance of a Grand Slam by not travelling to Ireland in 1972 because of the Troubles – and called it a day at the age of 27. He cut out early, denying himself a final chapter, written when most players are at their peak. Longevity is a virtue in this book, but somehow the premature retirement of Barry, the waywardness of his subsequent life with a drop too much taken, almost add to his lustre.

Barry John, the glider.

Rhys Priestland, a precocious playmaker at the 2011 World Cup.

Is it to be Phil? A curse on the bog of New Zealand, and hail the greatest try ever scored, by Gareth Edwards for the Barbarians against the All Blacks, gloriously started by Phil Bennett. If Barry thought in 1973 that nobody could ever be as good as himself, it was a miscalculation. Here was Barry Mark II, and not one for giving up. Phil put 1977 behind him and led Wales in 1978, scoring two tries in the Grand Slam decider against France.

Barry was a cruel player. Even now, when he talks of tormenting Fergie McCormick in the first Test of 1971, he laughs as he describes how he pushed the All Black full-back this way and then pulled him back that way. It was a game within a game and Barry loved being the puppet master that made a fool of an opponent. When, as runner, he left defenders sprawling he delighted in doing it with a minimum of movement, in order to maximize their embarrassment. And when they were behind him, he was likely to look back at them and put them down further with a quip. Phil would have apologised to Fergie. He would have gone back to a player that had clutched at this air and helped him to his feet.

Perhaps Barry at the age of 27 worked out that he was not going to become any more elusive, that from now on experience would be his guide. Where was the fun in wisdom? Perhaps he looked at the

Chin up! Phil Bennett dives over for the second of his two tries in the Grand Slam victory over France at Cardiff in 1978.

Right foot, left foot, whatever! Barry John demonstrates the virtue of twofootedness against France in 1972.

(Colorsport)

list of his victims and decided that there were now too many of them to evade with contempt. Perhaps retirement is an act of surrender as much as it is a farewell with fanfare. The moment Phil decided to finish was after a bruising, raw encounter against Ireland in 1978. Wales had won 20–16. He was sitting in the changing room at Lansdowne Road, looking around at a team that was too battered to celebrate, and he decided that enough was enough. This would be his last campaign.

Barry or Phil; Phil or Barry? It would be so easy to steer clear of the choice. I could say that although I never saw Percy Bush play – I just missed him in 1905 – I've heard so much about him and am going for him as a left-field selection. But that too would be an act of surrender. Hell, Barry or Phil?

I once asked Jonathan what he thought, and I know full well what he said. But I won't reveal his answer. I must do this on my own. Long ago, I wrote down my final, definitive, set-in-stone selection, and now I'm going to change my mind. The 10 shirt goes to Phil Bennett. And the pub erupts . . .

—OUTSIDE HALF—
10

'A kicking game second to none.'
Scrum-half Gareth Edwards pins the
Springboks back during the third Test of
the 1974 Lions series.   (Colorsport)

Chapter 6

9

SCRUM-HALF

'Unquestionably' is a dangerous word, one of those you slip in when you want to be done with an argument. It invites no challenge and is especially troublesome when delivered by someone you have already picked in your team, a rugby authority who might be assumed to speak with a certain weight. And so, when Bleddyn Williams, our 13, is on the record as saying that unquestionably the best scrum-half he ever saw was Haydn Tanner, it does rather take the tablet in which is etched the name of Gareth Owen Edwards and place it under a sledgehammer. This is an inconvenience, because some positions are supposed to be easier than others.

There is a further complication. I found myself on the campus of an institute of further education the other day, in the terrifying position of being surrounded by what can only be described as . . . young people.

Gareth in his element, taking on England at Cardiff in 1977.
(Colorsport)

I explained what I was doing, picking my best Welsh XV ever and they said: 'What a doddle.'

'Fair enough,' I said. 'But put three people on the case and you end up with three different answers.' There were about ten students around me. 'Give us a go, then,' they said. 'OK, who would you lot pick at scrum-half?'

Without a pause, ten voices chorused: 'Rob Howley.'

'Come on,' I said as condescendingly as possible. 'What about Gareth?'

'Gareth who?'

'Gareth Edwards.'

'Who's Gareth Edwards?'

Just as Bleddyn was influenced by Tanner – he had watched him in the 1930s, and then played with and against him in the 1940s – so the students preferred the scrum-half they had seen in the flesh. In that case, I feel in a creaking sort of way that I might press the case of Dicky Owen, who was the undisputed mastermind of the mighty Welsh team of the first dozen years of the twentieth century. It was Owen that initiated the move that led to the try by Teddy Morgan on the day Wales beat the All Blacks in 1905. Owen won 35 caps for Wales, a record that stood until Ken Jones broke it in 1955. He won five Triple Crowns with Wales in the championship of the four home nations, was captain on three occasions and was never afraid to make a point. Bemused by the refereeing of the scrum by Mr Findlay of Scotland in the Wales-England match of 1904, Owen let the England scrum-half put the ball in, even on the Welsh feed. He ran a pub in Swansea until he took his own life in 1932 at the age of 55.

Haydn Tanner played for Swansea against the All Blacks of 1935 while he was a pupil at Gowerton Grammar School. In fact, his half-back partner, Willie Davies, was still at school, too, at Gowerton County. Swansea won 11–3 and Jack Manchester, the All Back captain, issued a qualified statement to the press back home in New Zealand: 'Tell them we have been beaten, but don't tell them it was by a pair of schoolboys.'

That was in late September. Just before Christmas and while still 18, Tanner was picked to play for Wales, and was on the winning side again, 13–12. He went on the Lions tour to South Africa, but played in only one Test, through injury. The war then brought rugby to a halt for six years, but afterwards he played on for Wales until his last cap

Robert Howley

Dickie Owen

Haydn Tanner

Mike Phillips demonstrating Gareth's poacher's instinct, as he dives in for a try against Ireland in Cardiff.

Robert Howley sniping against South Africa.

Terry Holmes

David Bishop

against France in 1949. He had it all, a fine break, a wonderful pass and was indisputably, as underlined by Bleddyn Williams, one of the all-time greats.

As was Rob Howley. He had a long and accurate pass, was fast off the mark, could sidestep both ways and was tightly muscled in an age before compulsory pectoral definition. He flitted for a time between Bridgend and Cardiff, evidence of perhaps a lack of ruthlessness in his designs, and was injured on his two Lions tours, the winning one to South Africa in 1997 and the lost series of 2001 in Australia. He was a sensational athlete, but also thoughtful with his kicking and his decision-making. Injuries plagued him, however, and there always seemed to be doubts about whether he'd be available. The general sense of concern was reinforced by his slightly startled look and what looked like permanent worry lines on his brow. He would call it his natural mien and the furrows of concentration; others called him Stan, after Stan Laurel, as in Laurel and Hardy.

I think this – and I am back to being disgustingly patronising here, dear students – is what gives the scrum-half whose identity is unknown to you the edge over the unquestionably gifted Rob. Never once in his career of 53 caps for Wales, a span that included three Grand Slams in the Five Nations, did Gareth Edwards ever, ever give a hint of self-doubt. Strong as an ox, he walked into a changing room and everybody felt his confidence, and was uplifted by it. I know it sounds silly to adorn a rugby player with messianic qualities, but I have felt them: with Terry Holmes for Wales, and with David Bishop at Pontypool. There was something about these players at 9. They had presence.

It must have been hell for the scrum-halves who understudied Edwards through the 1970s: Ray 'Chico' Hopkins and Clive Shell, both far too good to play second fiddle for a decade. But Edwards denied them more than a sniff of the big time, durable of body as well as tungsten-tough of mind. He had a hamstring problem on the 1971 Lions tour of New Zealand and had to retire after ten minutes of the first Test, allowing Chico 70 minutes of glory, but Edwards was back for the second and back to his brilliant best for the third, when he seemed to hand off the entire Kiwi nation. New Zealanders save a special place for Sid Going, a ferocious competitor in his own right, but they admit in their own growling way, that Edwards was a bit special.

He won again with the Lions in South Africa in 1974. Admittedly they were great teams, but Gareth Edwards was the heart and soul of the entirety. He kept the forwards rumbling forward with a kicking game second to none, and he fed his outside halves, Barry John in New Zealand and Phil Bennett in South Africa, with a service that may not have been as slick as Robert Jones's, but was long enough to keep his 10s clear of danger. His pass was a bit like a laden jumbo jet – it needed a bit of a wind-up but once airborne could fly huge distances.

You can look at all the scrum-halves of yesterday and today and say that they have all had their moments. Mike Phillips had a grand Lions tour of South Africa in 2009 and rediscovered that form at the 2011 World Cup; Matt Dawson of England excelled when he replaced Rob Howley in 1997 and was all-important for England at the 2003 World Cup; Nick Farr-Jones and George Gregan were outstanding in all departments for Australia; Fourie Du Preez is perhaps the pick of the last half-dozen years, sniping and intelligent for South Africa. But none is Gareth Edwards. You can look at the rugby of 40 years ago and say it looks antiquated and slow. But not the way Edwards played it. He was so far ahead of his time that even the pass of the modern scrum-half has slowed down – the step, the look and then the release – to catch up with what he was doing all those years ago.

I feel guilty even dreaming of contradicting Bleddyn Williams and am sad to claim that I know better than the youth of today. But Gareth Edwards is unquestionably in the team.

Robert Jones, he of the slick service.

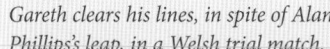

Gareth clears his lines, in spite of Alan Phillips's leap, in a Welsh trial match.

SCRUM-HALF

Seeing light on the blind side, Gareth needs no second opportunity at Cardiff in 1976. Scotland's Douglas Morgan (left) and Wales's Trevor Evans look on.

(Colorsport)

'A phenomenon.' Loose-head prop Gethin Jenkins steps in at scrum-half against Australia at Cardiff in 2010.

Chapter 7

1

LOOSE-HEAD PROP

It was tempting at first to put the props together, like the centres, because as far as I know they share certain skills, peculiar to what we call, in our ignorance, 'their world.' They are of a certain shape and they push and then they settle down in the company of others of their kind and talk in their own language about more pushing and what it is doing to the discs of their neck. Of course, there are other, more accessible, elements to their work, like boosting at the line-out, a job at which John Hayes, 6 feet 4 inches and more rocket launch-site than human, excelled, sending Paul O'Connell of Munster and Ireland into the air with a force known only to NASA.

You see, I have already drifted off the subject of Wales's best props. It is hard to concentrate, which is why I repeat that I was tempted to pool together numbers 1 and 3 and be done with them. This would

'The hooker tends to be a prop with attitude.' Garin Jenkins in a victorious Welsh dressing room, with New Zealand's World-Cup-winning coach, Graham Henry.

hark back to the days when roles were less defined and forwards simply had to have an all-round array of skills. This would give me a chance to mention Jehoida Hodges, if only for his name and the fact that he played in three Triple Crown (Grand Slam) teams of the early 20th century, and was a tight forward who sometimes filled in on the wing. In fact, I was more than tempted to throw in the hooker as well, because what he does is just as esoteric as the props. The hooker tends to be a prop with attitude. If any among you has ever wrapped your arms around a pair of barrels, thereby rendering yourselves defenceless, and plunged into a storm of heaving giants then you will recognise the terrifying claustrophobia of rugby's number 2 at the scrum. It is a position for the deranged, and I give you Brian Moore, Keith Wood and Garin Jenkins as living proof of what can happen to bright, articulate men who are sent to the sort of workplace that Victorian philanthropists spent their lives trying to eradicate. Of course, it could be that hookers go into the scrum by choice, which only confirms the suspicion that we may be able to study the human genome as light reading, but we still sometimes choose to drag our knuckles on the ground.

Charlie Faulkner leading Ireland a merry dance.

The easiest option was to herd 1, 2 and 3 together, call them the Pontypool front row and move on. Tony 'Charlie' Faulkner, Bobby Windsor and Graham Price. That would have done it, and even if Charlie had been forced out because of his lack of time on a Lions tour – he went as a replacement to New Zealand in 1977 – we could have gone for Staff Jones, also of Pontypool. Perhaps Staff was less mobile than, say, Clive Williams, Ian Stephens or Jeff Whitefoot, but he was utterly resistant to backward motion on the loose-head.

Then, however, two things happened. The first was that all this writing of the word 'Pontypool' seemed to trigger memories of being asked – as in ordered as a form of punishment: 'It'll be good for you.' – to go up into the second row by the one and only Ray Prosser, our coach and inspiration, and of spending many hours scrummaging, sometimes behind Charlie, sometimes behind Staff, more often behind Pricey, but always in the rain at the bottom end of Pontypool Park. And it came to me as a kind of repressed memory that I know a bit more about scrummaging than I really should, more than is natural.

Please bear with me; this won't take long. It's just that I hear a lot about angles of hips and height of shoulders nowadays, and how the arcane, recondite impenetrability of the scrum is threatening the good of the game. Well, I remember being issued with this as a technical manual: head up to straighten the back; bind as tight as you can, and

Wales's 2011 World Cup front row, Adam Jones, Huw Bennett and Gethin Jenkins.

Another of the modern loose-heads, Duncan Jones, driving low and hard at the Argentinians.

on the signal, heave until your eyes pop out. The complexity was condensed even further in Pross's argot: 'Edwoot, fucking push.'

It was an eight-man thing and nobody shirked. God, we loved scrummaging.

It was a speciality at Pontypool in the 1970s and in the wider world, as ruled by the Lions of that decade. The Lions of 1971, first with Ray McLoughlin and Sandy Carmichael, both injured in the Battle of Canterbury before the first Test, and then by the props that replaced them, Ian McLauchlan and Sean Lynch, brought a technical wit that unsettled the All Blacks. It was a decisive element in the

Cheered on by Stephen Jones (left), Gethin Jenkins is about to throw the ball away in celebration of his Grand Slam try against Ireland at Cardiff in 2005.

Gethin in Lions colours in New Zealand in 2005.

series that was won 2–1, with the final Test drawn. The Lions of 1974, with McLauchlan and Fran Cotton as props, went toe to toe with South Africa and won handsomely. The Lions of 1977, with Graham Price and Cotton, scattered the All Blacks at the scrum. The series would eventually be lost, but in Pontypool such an obliteration of the opposition scrum counted as a moral victory.

Do you remember me mentioning the four tries Gerald Davies scored against us in the Cup game at Pontypool? Every year in the late 1970s it seemed we were pulled out of the hat against Cardiff, and every year we would redouble our efforts at the scrum. One particular year, the game was due to be played when Wales lay for weeks beneath a blanket of snow and we were forced to find alternative training pitches. We turned up one Thursday night at Llanfrechfa Mental Hospital in a blizzard, and started lapping the grounds, illuminated by one single light bulb, flapping on top of a pole. Pricey looked up to see rows of people staring at us out of the windows. 'And we think they're mad,' he muttered.

Anyway, in the Gerald Davies tie we spent our customary amount of time on the scrum, and in particular trying to counteract the tendency of the Cardiff tight-heads – Mike Knill and John Dixon both gave us trouble over the years – to turn in, a classic defensive measure, under pressure from Charlie and Bobby on the Cardiff put-in. Pross worked on Charlie, telling him to use his outside arm to pull his opposite number by the shorts, even further out of the scrum, exposing him to a full broadside. Charlie was a master at judo and scarily good at all that grappling stuff. (He had also been a soldier in the Territorial Army. '*Alto las manos o tiro,*' he had shouted at people trying to sneak past his sentry post on Gibraltar. 'Hands up or I'll shoot.') If he perfected the manoeuvre and the rest of us timed our collective drive right, then a set of ribs would be vulnerable, the scrum would surge and the day would be ours. To hear bones crack was the aim of the day.

It didn't work. We never quite managed to crush the Cardiff scrum as we would have liked and the ball found its way to Gerald. I use it to illustrate the point that without the work of the prop there can be no strokes of genius on the wing.

The second thing that happened was Gethin Jenkins. He first played for Wales when he had just turned 23, in 2003 against Romania. This compares with Charlie who was first capped for Wales in 1975,

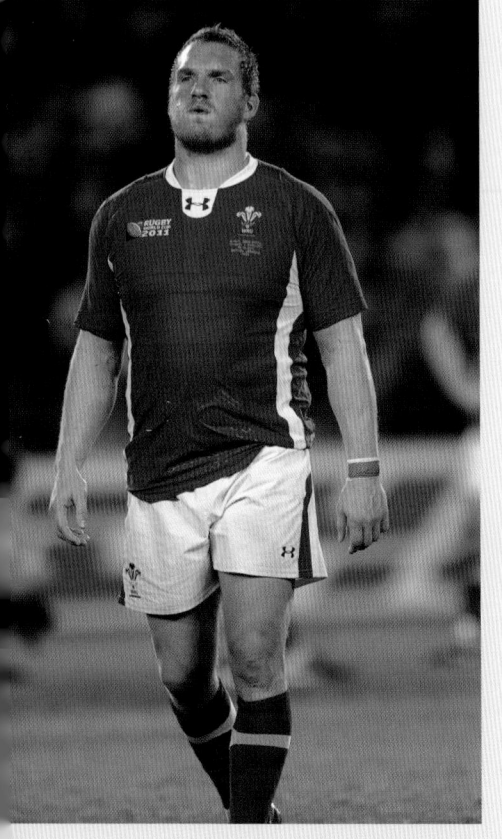

A reflective Gethin Jenkins, following defeat in the 2011 World Cup semi-final against France.

'This is the way to sidestep, Shane and Phil . . .'
Gethin Jenkins leads the attack against England
during the 2008 Grand Slam campaign.

age unknown, but estimated to be around the 34 mark. It wasn't the
only difference. In normal circumstances it would be right and proper
to view a prop who started as flanker and moved to the front row only
at the age of 15 with some suspicion. And a prop that professes to
this day not to care at all for scrummaging might have his union card
shredded. But Jenkins is a phenomenon, blessed with an engine that
seems impervious to aerobic stress. If he is a reluctant scrummager
he is still more than competent at the basic requirement of his craft,
and his contributions thereafter are priceless, in particular his tackle-
count. Never on the field of rugby has one player made so many tackles
beyond the call of duty. I know props have to cover certain guard
positions close to the breakdown, and might be expected to register
on the tackle tally there, as sorts of Greco-Roman wrestler, but Jenkins
pops up everywhere, the most enthusiastic scrambling defender in
open space.

He will reappear later as part of another story, and I must add that
he appears subject to a condition that will be explained later. But for
the moment it is enough to lay down the first name of the players on
whom everything depends, the forwards. Number 1, Gethin Jenkins.

LOOSE-HEAD PROP

'Not just a good fighter.'
Hooker Bobby Windsor follows
the ball against Argentina.

(Colorsport)

Chapter 8

2 HOOKER

I have already been flippant, if not downright rude, about hookers. This is only through ignorance. I know that they have opportunities to break out into daylight, because throwing into the line-out and then running behind the throw mean they can steal a march on the rest of the forwards if play goes infield. Matthew Rees, Dylan Hartley of England and Ross Ford of Scotland have their hands on the ball almost as much as their scrum-halves. And I know that some of them can be eminently sensible communicators and readers of the game. Because they have such a technically demanding set of duties – throwing and striking for starters – they can be as analytical as anyone. Robin McBryde was not just powerful of body in the front row, the strongest man in Wales, but he also now sits alongside Warren Gatland, another hooker, in the think-tank of the Welsh coaching set-up. Jonathan

'The strongest man in Wales,' Robin McBryde, Wales's forwards coach.

Matthew Rees, Welsh hooker and captain against England at Cardiff in 2011, chuckles his way through tackles.

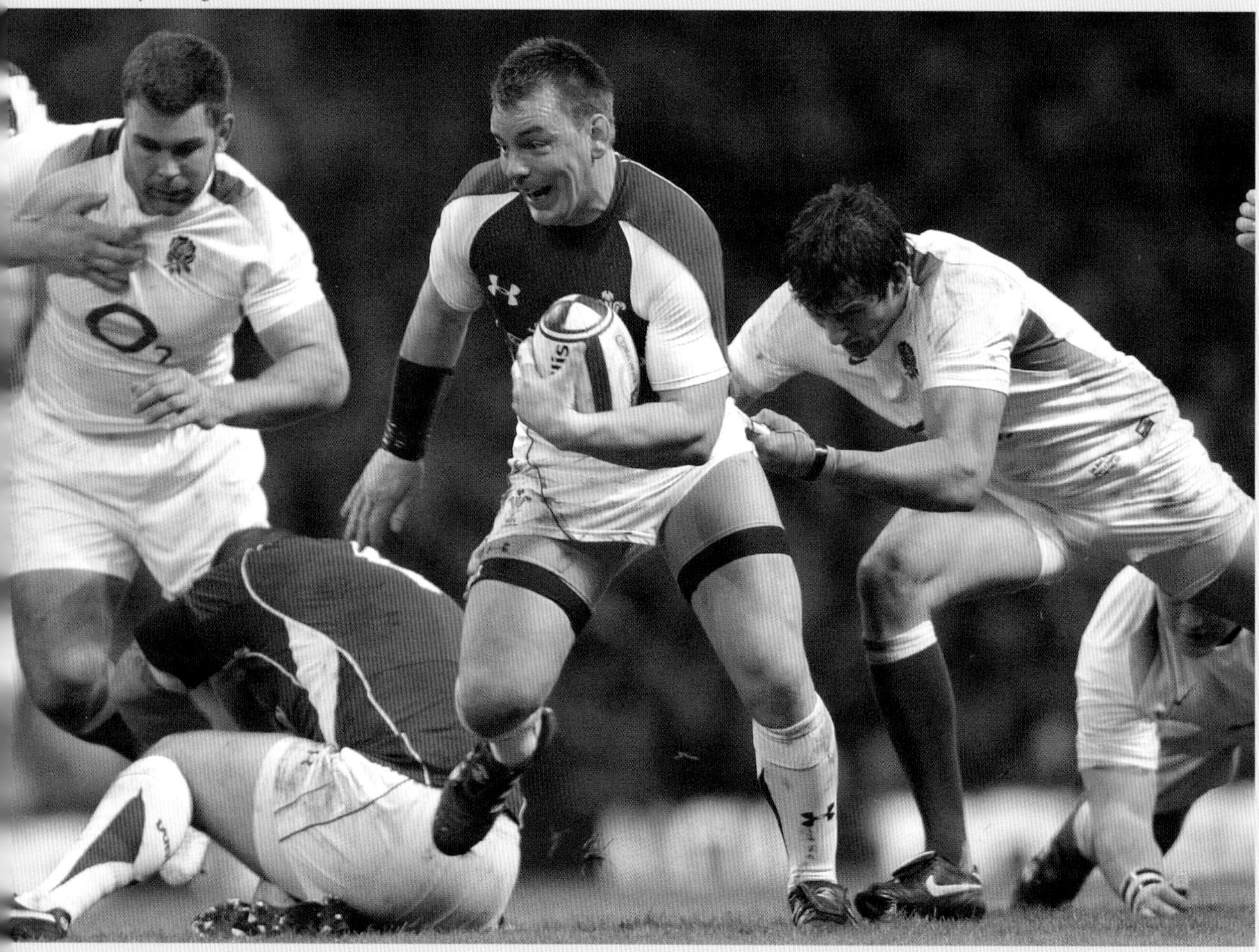

Humphreys was almost idiotically brave on the field for Cardiff and Bath and Wales, but makes nothing but sense when talking about – worrying about – the Ospreys.

There is nevertheless something of the night about hookers. Norman Gale, capped 25 times for Wales in the 1960s, was a wonderful servant of the game, as player, coach and chairman of Llanelli, but, my, he could glower. Jeff Young, 23 caps in the early 1970s, went from being perfectly sensible, they say, as a wing commander in the RAF to a player possessed, and not by the angels, when the whistle went for the start of a rugby game.

It is perhaps best to lean on the knowledge of others when it comes to the hooker. For someone who was a kindred spirit of Lucien Mias, in that they both espoused a creed of physical combat, Ray Prosser could be very sentimental about his rugby. He swore – and Pross swore a lot – that backs by nature were treacherous and that the only people you could trust in life were forwards. But when we went up north, in the days before Sale and Fylde and Waterloo decided that the Mias-Prosser method might have swayed a little too far from the physical towards total combat, he used to grow positively misty-eyed in the company of Malcolm Price. They had played together for Pontypool, Wales and the Lions in New Zealand in 1959. The centre had gone to play professional rugby league with Oldham in 1962, and when Prosser and Price met up in later years it was always a reunion of mythical proportions.

Price appeared to confirm the suspicion that if Pross had the occasional soft spot for backs of his time – for Benny Jones, cunning and impish at outside half, and Fenton Cole, so forceful on the wing that he was almost baptised a forward – he had time only for those that had worn the red, white and black of the Pooler. Again, this wasn't quite true, because if you ever wanted to see the girders that Pross wore as shoulders start to shake, all you had to do was ask him about Bryn Meredith.

Meredith played at hooker for London Welsh, but mostly for Newport, which should have caused him to be shunned by anybody from ten miles north. Up there, the view is that the town, port and now city of Newport form an alien gateway to the Eastern Valley. But Bryn was by birth from Abersychan, attached to the northern flank of Pontypool, and he went to school at West Mon in the town. He played 34 times for Wales and went on three Lions tours, to South Africa in 1955 and 1962, and to New Zealand in 1959, where he did not play a Test because the captain, Ronnie Dawson of Ireland, was also a hooker. It was said at the time, but never by the one that was missing out, that the wrong hooker was being selected. Because Bryn Meredith was an orchid in a forest of redwoods: a spring-heeled runner, a gifted handler of the ball, a gentleman. And Pross loved the way he played.

So, to oust Bryn from the hooker's position will take some doing. But Pross had another favourite, this one from Newport who came to play at Pontypool. Bobby Windsor, too, had a mean turn of pace and had excellent hands. But he was no orchid, and he was no gentleman. In the forest of redwoods, our Bob was a lumberjack armed with the biggest chainsaw you'll ever see.

Ray Prosser, Pontypool, Wales and Lions legend.   (Western Mail)

Bryn Meredith holds South Africa at bay for the Lions.

The Pontypool (and, in this case, Monmouthshire)
front row: (from the left) Graham Price, Bobby Windsor
and Charlie Faulkner. (Colorsport)

His time at the very peak of his powers was relatively short, from the summer of 1973, when he took over in the Welsh team from Jeff Young, to the summer of 1977. He went on the '74 Lions tour to South Africa as understudy to Irishman Ken Kennedy, but in fighting country Windsor was royalty. The Duke. In all the footage of the mayhem of that tour, as the Lions took the fight to the Springboks, there was not much proper boxing. There was a lot of flailing and swinging and it all looked pretty spectacular and savage, but connections, as against punches thrown, were few. Even Willie John McBride was more of the school of head-down and start-the-windmill. There were two exceptions: one a sort of air-to-ground missile, ripping in from thirty metres out, from full-back, JPR Williams. The other was Bob, calm as you like in the thick of it from the start, every punch counting. He was brutally efficient at being violent, and utterly cold-hearted about the whole business of pain. If Bobby could have been a merchant of agony, buying it and above all selling on at a profit, he would have been the richest man in rugby.

I am reminded (by the by, and nothing to do with Bob except that we are on the subject of suffering) of a story told to me by a Frenchman who happened to be drinking in the Bar Toulzac in Brive on the night of the famous fight in 1997 between the home club and the incoming players of Pontypridd. They had spent the afternoon engaged in a pulsating Heineken Cup tie, dotted with fights and other nefarious incidents. Now it was time to settle matters. According to my local witness, there was not one fight but two: first, a skirmish after which the small advance party of Pontyridd players withdrew to gather reinforcements; then the second battle of Brive. It was truly full-on, and if a lot of the action was of the inefficient rugby kind, it was supplemented by the use of all available furniture as heavy weaponry. And in the eye of this storm from the Wild West, the witness remembers seeing a vision of tranquillity. Dale 'The Chief' McIntosh, with not a bead of sweat on his brow, his tie never anything but elegantly tight around his neck, stood there, moving only to jab out an arm and despatch the next assailant.

Anyway, back to Bob. He was not just a good fighter, but also the force behind the Pontypool scrum, a supreme technician who worked with Charlie Faulkner against the tight-head on the opposition's feed. That is, loose-head Charlie and hooker Bob against the opposition number 3. The whole scrum used to quiver before the signal came to unleash the drive and then it would explode. People used to think it was one-dimensionally obsessive, but, blow me, it felt good. Bob was also the heart and soul of the driving maul, the look-out and navigator and then the outrider that would peel off with the ball and charge at some poor unfortunate.

To be honest, there were hookers who could throw in better. Mike Watkins and Alan Phillips could find Bob Norster unerringly at Cardiff; Billy James never missed Allan Martin at Aberavon. Bob had a sort of shot-putt of a throw, which generated as much wobble as rifling turn. 'I chuck it, you catch it,' was his reply if his jumpers asked for a change of flight. This was a variation on one of Barry John's lines. When asked by any scrum-half how he would like the ball delivered unto him – high, low, left or right – the King replied: 'You pass it, I'll catch it.' The Duke gave this a bit of spin, which was more than he did to the ball.

Former international hooker Alan Phillips, manager of the Welsh team at the 2011 World Cup.

Bob went on the Lions tour of 1977 and lost his place to Peter Wheeler of England, one of the greats in his own right. By then, Bob's back was beginning to give him trouble – he'd end up in traction in Panteg Hospital. He continued to play after all the weights and pulleys were removed, but lost his international place after burning himself on a lime cocktail used to mark the lines one day. His back was a bubbling sea of blisters. With his best days behind him, he played on, filling in at prop, folding himself less aggressively into the scrum, but still a marvel at the mechanical exercise. He would limp on to the field for the 1983 WRU cup final against Swansea and earn himself a winner's medal.

Huw Bennett, the hooker who exceeded all expectations for Wales at the 2011 World Cup.

He was never one to give anything but an honest view. The 1975 victory for Wales against France has gone down in folklore for all sorts of reasons: Phil Bennett being dropped for newcomer John Bevan, who had a sensational match at outside half and made a tackle in the corner to rival any of JPR's; the last win in Paris for 24 years; the fact that Wales introduced five other new caps for the game, including Charlie Faulkner and Graham Price. It was the first time the Pontypool front row played together for Wales. It was a stunning 25–10 win over the country that challenged Wales for supremacy in the 1970s, another in the series of clashes between the giants of European rugby. 'Nah,' Bob would mutter in his gravelly voice, 'we beat them because they were rubbish.'

We, Pontypool this time, were once preparing on a less glamorous weekend to play against Aberavon, sitting in the away changing room at the Talbot Athletic Ground, never an easy place for us. This is where

With all the finesse of an Edwards or Bennett, Bobby Windsor puts boot to ball at Murrayfield in 1979. Allan Martin (4) may well be regretting his decision to pick up. (Colorsport)

David Bishop broke a bone in his neck. 'He'll be all right; he's just hamming it up as usual,' we said when we saw him in a heap. We weren't wrong; it's just that it took him more than a year to prove us right. But even before we lost the player that would transform us from a forward-based side to, well, a one-man team, it was something of a jinxed venue for us. I was trying to persuade everyone that it was time to break the hex, that much as we loved to play at Pontypool Park, to appreciate the delights of home we had to be able to travel away and grind out victories. It was a Saturday afternoon like any other, a pitch like any other. 'It's 3 o'clock, this is our time,' I said.

'Aye,' growled our veteran hooker, 'And roll on half past four.' And out he trotted to do his incomparable stuff. The number one number two: Bobby Windsor. I should also like to give him full licence to nag at Gethin Jenkins. This is the condition on which the loose-head prop's selection depends: that he listens to his hooker and commits himself one hundred per cent to the scrum. And not necessarily because all that hard work per se is so very vital to the spinning of the earth on its axis, but because I should merely advise Gethin that it makes for an altogether easier life to stay on the right side of our Bob.

HOOKER

With his 'giant pair of lungs,' tight-head prop Graham Price keeps going during the fourth Lions Test in New Zealand in 1983.

(Colorsport)

Chapter 9

3

TIGHT-HEAD PROP

Gethin Jenkins arrived on the Wales scene at the tender age of 21 years and 11 months. Tender, that is, for a prop. Graham Price was 23 and considered a bairn when he was launched into one of the most intimidating scrummaging environments on the planet, the Parc des Princes, where France played their internationals between the age of the Stade Colombes and the Stade de France. The Parc des Princes is a barnacle stuck to the Boulevard Périphérique, the ring-road around the centre of Paris. The concrete bowl used to rock to the rugby blast brought up to the capital from the southern half of France, and every sign of weakness in the opposition was greeted with a trumpet fanfare, an 'Olé' and a 55,000-strong shriek of derision. It was no place for the faint of spirit, or for the weak of scrummaging power.

Pricey had been packing down for Pontypool since he was 18 and

Graham Price has New Zealand's Sid Going in his sights at Christchurch in the second Test of the 1977 Lions series. (Colorsport)

had served a tough apprenticeship, trudging back up the hill for home after matches in his teenage years, too bent out of shape to face more than a couple of pints of orange squash in the clubhouse. He had been a centre in his early teens, before he was ordered to be the cornerstone of the scrum. Here he was, still slim of waist, being asked to lock up a scrum that at the time was being shoved all over South Wales. These were the early days of the coaching reign of Ray Prosser, before Bobby and Charlie swept into town, a time when Pontypool were bottom of the pile.

The front row by 1975 had turned, almost literally, the scrum around. They had certainly swapped reverse gear for forward motion, and their reward was to be picked for the first time as an ensemble – as they certainly did not say on Pontypool Park – for Wales's away game in Paris. Now, Bob has already been quoted on the subject of how poor France were that day, but it was a view on general play. The confrontation up front was still brutal. The scrummaging, as always, came first and it was a savage test of endurance. There was no expectation for a debutant 23-year old to do anything but the basics.

And yet it remains one of the enduring sights of the golden age of the 1970s, the blond-haired Price setting off in the closing moments after a kick downfield from the Welsh 22. True, he was overtaken by J.J. Williams in the hot pursuit of the ball, but Pricey still kept running, the ball eventually sitting up sweetly for him, and not the wing, to dive over. The game was already won, but this was to be a try that immortalised a player, his front-row union and his club. The legend of the Pontypool front row was born.

Pricey remained throughout his career a wasp-waisted prop, an athlete who sometimes had to take the scrum low to divert the opposition drive into a downward force. He was never quite the cold-hearted executioner that Bobby and Charlie could be. It wasn't Pricey that prompted the *Western Mail* to label Pontypool the Viet Gwent. He had instead a giant pair of lungs and a speed that no other prop could match, until the arrival of Gethin Jenkins. He also had hands made for catching any old rubbish slapped down to him as he peeled around the back of the line-out. 'You flap it; I'll catch it,' might have been his version of the old line.

He set a record as the most capped prop for Wales, with 41 appearances, and went on three Lions tours, in 1977, 1980 and 1983. His place in the team of these pages would have been absolutely nailed down had it not been for the emergence of an entirely different species of tight-head prop, Adam Jones.

David Young, looking as a prop should look.

Phil Vickery, England and Lions tight-head.

Billy Williams

The dark-haired one of the coiled Neath twin-set – Duncan Jones being the blond – was younger than Graham Price when he was first capped by Wales in 2003. But at 22, he was entirely different of shape, his waist more that of a contented ruminant than a wasp. This is how props should look, like Stuart Evans and David Young, both of whom deserve more than this as an acknowledgement. Perhaps it is because they both went north in their prime, or perhaps because Adam Jones made the modern position his. Hefty, he could still shift over a short distance, a burst on the wing, complete with graceful dive and glide, providing him with his first try for Wales. He was not, however, considered to be a marathon runner. In fact, when Steve Hansen was coach of Wales, he was confined to cameo roles: half an hour here at most, twenty minutes more the norm there. Come to think of it, his whole career seemed to be doing little more than trundling along until Graham Price, in his *Western Mail* column in the autumn of 2008, pointed out that the Welsh scrummage was holding up pretty well, and if you were secure on your own put-in it was because the tight-head prop in particular was doing his job.

Still, it was something of a surprise when he was selected for the 2009 Lions tour to South Africa, and he was perhaps something of a shock pick for the bench, ahead of Euan Murray of Scotland, for the first Test in Durban. Phil Vickery would be the starting tight-head, as universally predicted, to face Tendai 'The Beast' Mtawarira. A press conference was held in a school up the coast before that all-important opening encounter with the Springboks and Adam was one of several players put up for interview. He was not exactly the centre of attention, and only a couple of Welsh rugby writers sat down with him, more to keep him company than conduct a formal question and answer. He took it all in is stride. He knew the way these things worked; he'd been around a bit.

The Lions were hammered at the scrum on the Saturday. Somehow, the Beast had the absolute number of Phil Vickery and the Springbok forwards used this springboard to drive their way into a huge lead. Replacements had to be made, and so it was that the spare hooker, Matthew Rees, and the back-up prop, Adam Jones, trotted on to pack down alongside Gethin Jenkins and become the first all-Wales front row for the Lions since Courtney Meredith, Bryn Meredith and Billy Williams in the entire series against South Africa in 1955.

And at this point I should just like to ruin any dramatic tension by saying that the two props from that drawn series of '55 were much respected, and their achievement should be noted. Any record that

Adam Jones, a world-class prop.

Adam Jones, Matthew Rees and Gethin Jenkins, the first all-Wales Lions front row since 1955.

Graham Price sniffs the try line against Ireland in 1977. (Colorsport)

stands for 54 years has to put its holders into the reckoning, and the only reason Meredith C. and Williams W.O.G. have been overlooked is simple mathematics: their 14 and 22 caps respectively against the 41 of Price and the combined tallies of Jones and Jenkins that are soaring beyond 70. It could be argued that in 1955 it took ages to accumulate 20 caps, but that is where the selection process can be cruel.

And at this point, I should also like to pay tribute to Rees, who did not even receive a mention in the hooker's slot. He was excellent on the Lions tour of 2009 and took to the role of captain of Wales with natural authority. The only reason he does not feature more strongly is that he is still very much a work in progress and will have plenty of opportunities in the near future to muscle his way in.

And it is at that this selfsame point that I should like to mention the try scored by Gethin Jenkins in the Grand Slam game against Ireland in 2005. He charged down Ronan O'Gara's punt on the Irish 10-metre line, stayed on his feet, got to the ball first, delicately kicked it ahead and won the race for the line. I didn't want to mention it before Graham Price's effort against France in 1975, because I wanted to bracket the props together as, well, a pair of freaks, really. Both have to be lumps by design, but they are both aerobically over-endowed, both completely at ease in open spaces far removed from the slog of their propping routines.

And now we can return to the moment when Messrs Jones, Rees and Jenkins are united as the Lions front row in Durban in 2009. The game is doomed, and before they know it the entire Lions pack is being rolled back in a giant maul. Except it isn't all over. The scrum is mended by the new unit, and from 26–7 down an astonishing recovery begins. Eventually the Springboks hold out to win 26–21, but Adam Jones is now a world-class prop, a central plank of the tour. The rock of Wales. How he was missed when he limped off with a calf injury in the 2011 World Cup semi-final against France.

By then, his place as cornerstone of the entire Welsh team was established. In 2009 he was working on it. In the second Test at Loftus Versfeld in Pretoria, one of the biggest cheers on a day of record decibels from the mouths of travelling supporters, was for Jones as he won a penalty against the Beast at a scrum five metres from the Lions line. The Lions were in superb form, dominant up front and scintillating behind. They were in complete control, until, that is, both centres, Jamie Roberts and Brian O'Driscoll, and both props, Adam Jones and Gethin Jenkins, were forced off through injury. Jones was cleaned out by Bakkies Botha, the South African second row who was not inclined to enter rucks with much consideration for the welfare of anybody in his path. Flying lock met stationary prop and snap went a shoulder. Asked if he felt he was taken out illegally, Jones later shrugged: 'No, I got it wrong. I should have seen him coming.'

With both props off the field, the set piece reduced to a state of inertia. Uncontested scrums are one of the curses of the game. Free possession from one such huddle granted the Springbok wing, Bryan Habana, a gap in midfield, an area now barely patrolled by a concussed O'Driscoll. It was the Springboks' turn to mount a remarkable comeback. They won 28–25, Jaque Fourie scoring a try and Morné Steyn landing a kick from halfway to earn praise for themselves and make life uncomfortable for Ronan O'Gara, the replacement who missed a tackle on the centre and gave away the penalty. If it was not the Irishman's finest five minutes, just as important was the loss of the two Welsh props earlier, underlining the value of unseen forces in the public spectacle.

Price or Jones? A pair from Pontypool, Faulkner and Price, or two from the new order, Jenkins and Jones? I am afraid I am swayed by nostalgia, by the memory of a grunted instruction: 'More weight, Edwoot,' and in goes Graham Price.

———————————— TIGHT-HEAD PROP ————————————

With 'the most unbelievable standing jump', Lions second-row forward Robert Norster competes for possession against Australia in 1989.　(Colorsport)

Chapter 10

4 & 5

THE SECOND ROW

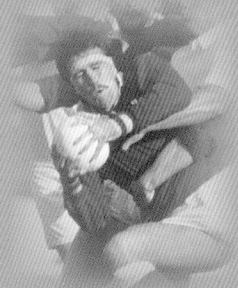

I have doubled up the second-row positions, because there are similarities here in their duties and because 4 and 5 tend to go together as a pair: Geoff Wheel and Allan Martin of Wales in the 1970s; David Marques and John Currie, or Paul Ackford and Wade Dooley of England, Bakkies Botha and Victor Matfield of South Africa. They are the biggest players on the field, bound to push, receive kick-offs, hit rucks hard, drive the ball forward without fuss and generally ooze menace. The French locks down the years, from Lucien Mias to the Spanghero brothers – Walter and Claude, who spent as much time feuding with each other as anyone outside the family – to Michel Palmié, Alain Estève, Jean-François Imbernon, Jean Condom and Olivier Merle, have generally secreted more menace than most, although you start a scrap with the Argentina second rows at your peril.

The long arm of the law. Robert Norster (right) tussles with England's Wade Dooley at Cardiff in 1987.

Luke Charteris, outstanding for Wales at the 2011 World Cup.

John Perkins, who was never the biggest in the second row for Pontypool and Wales but who was armed with a sweet left, always said that against really big meat-eaters you had to save yourself for the one shot and pray that it would be good enough. He had for years a running battle with John Morgan of Maesteg and Bridgend, again not the biggest, but one tough hombre. Perk admitted that he had not always come out on top. In fact, if he didn't make an impression next time, he might have to concede defeat. There was an honour about these things, and after another afternoon of shoving and obstructing and threatening and cursing down the front of the line-out, Perk felt that now was the moment and gave it his all. There was a connection. We all heard it, but nobody fell. Perk groaned. We all heard it. And then, slowly, the mighty Morgan sagged to his knees. He had been caught on a nose that had been broken in the previous game. It was with some relief that Perk heard his rival was about to emigrate to Zimbabwe.

There are, however, differences between the second rows, too, particularly at the line-out, with 4 being, as above, more the grappler at the front and 5 more graceful in the middle (Dooley and Ackford, both of the police force, were the exception to prove the rule, with Inspector Ackford the more refined, despite jumping at the front, and Constable Dooley a tad more heavyweight in the middle). Wales in their Grand Slam seasons of 2005 and 2008 neatly found combinations to fit the bill of enforcer and thoroughbred: Brent Cockbain and Robert Sidoli; Ian Gough and Alun Wyn Jones. There is every chance that Bradley Davies will become one of those whose presence on the team-sheet offers reassurance to the nation.

Alun Wyn might be there already, for he is as fine a physical specimen as has taken up residency in the engine room. He is athletic and more than fast enough for the position, even if he did not quite have the legs in the closing minutes of the game against New Zealand in November 2009 to go the full length of the field. That would have been too much to ask, although he took it badly that he hadn't pulled off the impossible. It's good to know that he sees no bounds to his contributions. If there is a problem it comes elsewhere, with a strange tendency for one so bright and devoted and with normally such a safe pair of hands to make mistakes at just the wrong moment, like dropping a simple restart, or hanging out a leg to trip up Dylan Hartley at Twickenham in 2010. I suppose we have to accept that if there are

'Gwlad, gwlad . . .'
Alun Wyn Jones, flanked by Jamie Roberts (right),
Leigh Halfpenny and Gareth Cooper, lives the
National Anthem.

Geoff Wheel, mauling powerhouse.

Robert Norster (right) and Ian Stephens (left) congratulate the author on his try against France in 1984.   (Colorsport)

medics like JPR and Jamie Roberts who have a complete disregard for their own well-being there will have to be lawyers like Alun Wyn who are irresistibly drawn to crossing the legal divide.

The names tumble out, but there is a problem with these positions of 4 and 5, and it seems to have something to do with the Lions, where no Welsh pair in half a century has left an indelible mark. Now, this may be unfair on Geoff Wheel, who was cruelly denied a place on the 1977 tour to New Zealand, on which the tourists most certainly did leave an impression up front. The tic that never stopped him from being a mauling powerhouse for Swansea and Wales was deemed too serious for air travel. And we think health and safety are a bane only of the 21st century. But even if he had been allowed to go on tour, would he have recaptured overseas the understanding he had with Martin for Wales? Panther, as Allan was known, looked as if he was not exactly designed for jumping, since his legs seemed to have been made for someone less developed up top, but he had sprung heels and launched himself to 34 caps for Wales. He played well in tandem with an established partner: with Wheel for Wales, and Billy Mainwaring, another international player, at Aberavon. We shall never know if Wheel and Martin would have worked for the Lions, but there must be doubts. Panther played in the first Test in 1977, alongside Moss Keane of Ireland, but the combination that worked for the Lions as the series unfolded and as they pushed the New Zealand All Blacks from South Island to North was Bill Beaumont and Gordon Brown.

In fact, if it is hard to find a successful Welsh pair of second-row Lions, it is difficult to find a single Welsh lock to have prospered as an individual Lion. Keith Rowlands played in three Tests in 1962 and scored a try in the final one, but his international career for Wales only lasted five caps. A few others with a longer domestic record were handed the Lions shirt, like Martin, at the start. There was Alun Wyn in 2009 in South Africa, Bob Norster in New Zealand in 1983 and Australia in 1989. But by the end of the series a different combination had come to the fore: Simon Shaw and Paul O'Connell in '09, Steve Bainbridge and Maurice Colclough in '83, and Ackford and Dooley in '89. A list of those that have excelled on Lions tours of the past 35 years show that England and the second row go very well together: Beaumont, Colclough, Bainbridge, Ackford, Dooley, Martin Bayfield, Martin Johnson, Danny Grewcock, Ben Kay and Simon Shaw.

England's Martin Johnson outjumped by Gareth Llewellyn.

2005 Grand Slam second-row combination Brent Cockbain (above) and Robert Sidoli gang up on New Zealand scrum-half Justin Marshall at the 2003 World Cup.

Victor Matfield advances.

Of those, Johnson would vie with Colin Meads for a place at 4 in my all-time world team. The mighty All Black might claim to have taught Johnson a thing or two when the Leicester youngster went out to Te Kuiti in King Country for some life experience. I don't suppose they played much classical harp together, but Johnson ended up playing for New Zealand Under 21s. I think they rather wanted to keep him. Instead, he returned home and led the Lions in 1997 and 2001, and England to Grand Slam glory in the Six Nations and to world victory in 2003. By the time of the tournament in Australia in '03 the sparkle had gone out of many of the England players, including in the early stages Jonny Wilkinson. Not Johnson. He hoisted England on his back and carried them to victory. The only way to decide between him and Meads would be to place them in a boxing booth and pick the one to emerge on two feet.

For a partner, I would invite John Eales and Victor Matfield to discuss which of them should wear the number 5 shirt, perhaps over a fine bottle of Australian or South African wine. They'd probably argue more over the label than their selection, and might end up agreeing to share games. Take your pick, but it might be handy to have Eales as a reserve kicker. Not that he was the first place-kicking second row, for Allan Martin had scored for Wales with his toe-on style.

I digress, which may not allay your fears that I am being a bit churlish about second rows from Wales. I apologise and recognise that even those that did not last the course of a Lions tour were very fine players. It might be added that Wales's most capped second row, Gareth Llewellyn, was never selected for a Lions tour. In the accumulation of 92 caps, under no fewer than eight different coaches of Wales, he instead went to three World Cups.

I suppose, however, that being a Lion remains something of a portal. Brian Price of Newport played in two Tests against Australia and in the first against New Zealand in 1966 . . . but I keep bumping into the problem of keeping going and leaving a lasting impression. The word of the time in New Zealand was that the Lions led by Mike Campbell-Lamerton were there to be taken, especially up front, and this hardly encouraged any Kiwi players to go easy on them.

Also on that tour of 1966 was Delme Thomas of Llanelli. He played in the second Test, thereby winning a Lions cap before being selected for Wales. Remarkably, he played in the second Test as a prop. Nobody would have more first-hand experience of the demands of playing against New Zealand in New Zealand. He toured South Africa with the Lions in 1968 and was part of the great team of 1971, playing in the first two Tests. Now he could claim to have beaten New Zealand in New Zealand, which would have been the pinnacle of most players' careers, but which was topped in Delme's case when he led his beloved Llanelli to victory at Stradey Park over the All Blacks in 1972.

With his sleeves rolled up high and bare arms reaching even higher over the line-out, Delme was an icon of the Welsh game and Welsh-speaking sport. If sentiment were the lubricant of this team, its embrocation, his name would be written down first, smudged by a tear. But an old nagging doubt presents itself, the reminder that for the deciding Tests of 1971 Gordon Brown was selected alongside Willie John McBride.

Part of me wants to forget the Lions in this position and make it more internal. Go for a number 4, say, who satisfies the enforcer criteria essential in Welsh rugby, ahead of being classy enough for a tour. Brian Thomas knocked a few about in the 1960s, the most feared of a Neath pack that marauded its way through the fixture lists of that decade. Or I could pick Ray Prosser at the front of the line-out, where

Delme Thomas and Brian Price, separated by Gareth Edwards.

Ireland and the Lions' Willie-John McBride, one of the all-time greats.

R. H. Williams rises highest against Ireland in 1959, with Ray Prosser behind him.

(Western Mail)

Roy John won plaudits everywhere.

(Western Mail)

he played for Pontypool, rather than at prop where he played for Wales and the Lions in 1959. A little bit of terror never harmed anyone – except of course it did.

Since, however, we are going backwards in time, we may as well keep going. And deep in the 1950s we come across three names – a pair and a single – that satisfy all the conditions. In 1950 Roy John was selected for Wales in the second row instead of his club-mate at Neath, Rees Stephens. Either at number 8 or in the second row, Stephens is a bit unlucky not to make the shortlist, but John was an instant success, playing in Wales's Grand Slam of that year, going on the Lions tour to New Zealand and winning plaudits everywhere for his athleticism at the line-out. He would play in Wales's second Grand Slam of that decade, in 1952 and in the Wales team that beat the All Blacks in Cardiff in 1953.

With him in the first two Tests in New Zealand in 1950 was Don Hayward, born in Pontypool but a player for Newbridge. Hayward was like Pross in that he could double up as both a prop and a lock. John went the other way in the rows of the forwards, being selected behind Hayward in the third Test as a wing forward. If they could have been united for the fourth in glory it might have been a different story, but Hayward was considered to be worn out by the end of the tour, having played in 18 games, and John packed down in the second row with Ireland's Jimmy Nelson. The Lions went down 11–8 to lose the series 3–0, with the first Test drawn. The trail for the perfect pair has gone a bit cold.

The biggest impression was made by Rhys 'RH' Williams later in the decade. Or at least his play made an impression, if not his surname. Colin Meads told me that one of the best opponents he ever faced was in his early days, against 'a bloke named Rhys.' Meads started back in 1957, and I had to check whether it was Rees as in Stephens, or Rhys as in Williams. It was on the Lions tour of 1959, Williams's second tour – he played in ten consecutive Lions Tests from 1955 to '59 – and the young Meads set about putting the son of Cwmllynfell off his game. 'I tried everything,' said Meads, which covers a multitude of sins, 'but the bastard never wavered once. I learned such a lesson about the powers of concentration you need.'

For Meads, incidentally, the biggest goal of the early part of his career as a touring All Black was not to beat South Africa, as is traditionally held to be the stiffest challenge for New Zealanders, but Wales, specifically in Cardiff. The All Blacks lost against Wales in 1905, 1935 and 1953. The Invincibles, as the tourists of 1924–25 were known, did win, but in Swansea. In short, New Zealand had never beaten Wales in Cardiff. That record was put straight in December 1963, and has not had a chink put in it since.

Anyway, in the final Test of the 1959 tour, Williams won the last six line-outs and the Lions, who had earned the respect of New Zealand with the invention of their back play, won their one and only Test of the series thanks to the efforts of their Welsh second row. That is good enough for me, and R.H. Williams is selected at 4.

Alongside him could easily slip the other second row of the 1950s, Roy John. But it must have been that snippet about six line-outs on the trot, and suddenly we are fast-forwarding to a different decade, into the inglorious early 80s. And it is here that I hear an ironic cheer at Twickenham, not for an unexpected pair of drop goals by Malcolm Dacey, but for a line-out won by England. 1984, made into the stuff of nightmares by George Orwell, and not so good for the England team

RH more spring-heeled than the Springboks.

Robert Norster secures possession against England at the 1987 World Cup, in spite of Peter Winterbottom's attentions.

(Colorsport)

Norster and Dooley continue their dispute at Cardiff.

as Bob Norster sends back a stream of ball to Terry Holmes on their throw. There is able assistance, from John Perkins at the front, and from Richard Moriarty directly behind him, but it is Bob's moment, and there he is, soaring, raining ball down from the top of his leap. He had the most unbelievable standing jump, leaving an entire airspace between his feet and the ground. When England eventually scrambled the ball from a line-out down to Steve Smith, the crowd let out that cheer, and the scrum-half promptly kicked it back into touch, where Bob began his winning ways all over again.

OK, he could be slightly fastidious and sometimes when he perceived that it was not going to be his day, nothing could persuade him otherwise. OK, he never quite overwhelmed the southern hemisphere as he did Twickenham. He liked a minimum of contact and would therefore require a specialist protection unit around him. But I think that could be arranged, because Bob Norster on his good days was a sight to behold, a self-raising defiance of gravity. And I think he would only be at his most feline among a cast designed to bring out the very best in each other.

THE SECOND ROW
4 & 5

'An outstandingly good player.'
Blind-side wing forward Jeff Squire (second from the left)
closes ranks in the Welsh line-out, alongside Derek Quinnell
and Allan Martin, against France in 1978.

(Colorsport)

Chapter 11

6

BLIND-SIDE WING FORWARD

There's something appealing about the anonymity of the number 6 shirt, although perhaps it's not anonymity but invisibility in the role of the unseen stalker, the flanker who has to grovel and scrape on the ground, and tie up the short side, snuffing out any probe there before anyone has a chance to get up a head of steam and break out into full public gaze. The best I ever saw was Richard Hill of England, although I have a suspicion that Dan Lydiate may soon be challenging for a permanent place in our affections. What did Hill ever do? Well, nothing at first glance, but then you would watch again and he was everywhere, somehow making three tackles in ten seconds, acting as the tiniest link in a long chain with a slipped pass or simply being there, anywhere, at the right time. It is the most selfless position on the field. I still think that if Hill had not gone off concussed in the second

Test of the Lions tour of 2001, taken out by centre Nathan Grey, the outcome of that series might have been different. As it was, Australia won an utterly absorbing threesome of games 2–1.

Alan Whetton of the 1987 New Zealand side was also excellent, the broom that would tidy up after the open-side, Michael Jones, had swept forward, the hand that would straighten the furniture after it had been scattered by number 8, Wayne Shelford. Or perhaps he was the drill that made the first hole, so that his back-row colleagues could have a full blast. Mark Shaw of an earlier generation of All Blacks was another, or Alex Wyllie . . . they churn out these masters of good housekeeping in New Zealand, although 'Grizz' Wyllie could introduce an element of anarchy as well. Jean-Claude Skrela of France made the invisible visible for France in the 1970s, the perfect complement to Jean-Pierre Rives and Jean-Pierre Bastiat.

Nobody fitted the bracket of serving without fuss the needs of others better than the third man of a famous Welsh back row: Mervyn Davies, John Taylor and Dai Morris. Dai, the miner from Rhigos, a ghostly presence in a formidable Neath pack, was as slim and fast on the field as a whippet. And so quiet and modest off it that he would be utterly incapable of telling you how gifted he was. He was above all an intelligent player, a solver of problems, a facilitator so that others might prosper. Part of his famous invisibility is nevertheless based on the fact that he was never selected for the Lions and at this late stage – we are in the back row – it is not easy to resist a rising indignation, an inclination to register a protest vote and make a selection to right an injustice.

But on the Lions tour of 1971 the player chosen ahead of him was also Welsh, and it is equally hard to think of publishing a Welsh team without acknowledging the dynasty of the Quinnells. Derek, pater familias, was uncapped by Wales in '71, but he was one of the biggest success stories of a tour that overflowed with tales of gambles that paid off. He struggled with his knee on the early part of the tour but, with the series standing at 1–1, he was brought in on the blind side to help manage the threats posed by a particular pair of opponents, wing forward Ian Kirkpatrick and scrum-half Sid Going. It was a blocking brief executed to perfection. The Lions won the third Test 13–3. The series could not now be lost. Quinnell's knee flared up again and he slipped once more out of the reckoning. But as brief contributions go, it had been anything but anonymous.

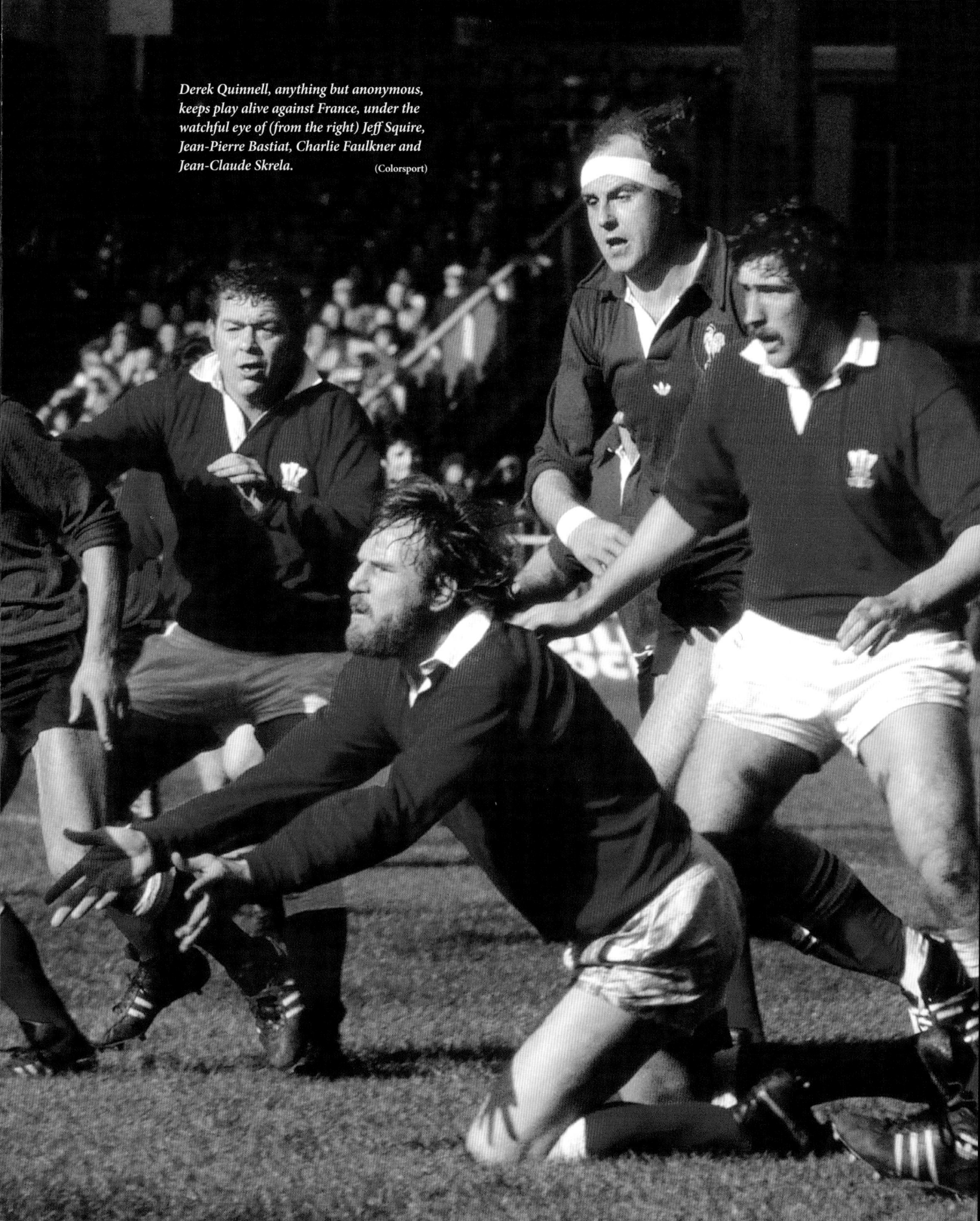

Derek Quinnell, anything but anonymous, keeps play alive against France, under the watchful eye of (from the right) Jeff Squire, Jean-Pierre Bastiat, Charlie Faulkner and Jean-Claude Skrela. (Colorsport)

Dan Lydiate, a serious challenger for a permanent place in our affections.

Ryan Jones, a player of many positions, and Grand Slam captain in 2008.

Colin Charvis on the charge at the 2003 World Cup, urged on by Adam Jones.

And that's the trouble with this notion of the quiet toiler. Another contender would be Colin Charvis who, like Morris and Quinnell, could also play at number 8. But it's hardly an invisible hand that scores 22 tries in international rugby, a world record for a forward. And if there is an attraction in the protest vote for Morris there is the appeal of selecting Charvis the rebel. Over the course of his 94 caps for Wales he rarely seemed out of trouble, a constant thorn in the side of authority. When the regions of Wales were formed in 2003–04 season, somehow the captain of Wales at the World Cup of '03 found himself unattached to any of the new franchises. Off he went, instead, on some grand tour, to Tarbes in France, then Newcastle in England before resettling in Wales with the Newport Gwent Dragons. The harshest treatment of this wanderer – even more disturbing than being knocked clean out by Jerry Collins of the All Blacks – came when he was caught, fleetingly, with a rueful smile on his face on the day Wales lost to Italy in Rome in that weird year of '03, and he was denounced in a nasty little smear campaign. He never deserved that.

There are two other contenders. No, three, because I should like to slip Ryan Jones in as a challenger at 6, if only because he will not make the shortlist at number 8. Perhaps he will end his playing days as a major player in the second row. At the very least we shall remember him as a player of many positions, but I should like to underline here the contribution he made from the blind side in the Six Nations Grand Slam of 2005 and from across the back row on the Lions tour of the same year. After the Lions left New Zealand in 1993 there was a review of the visitors to have impressed their hosts up front. They said there was only one Lion they would like to keep, Ben Clarke of England. In 2005, it was almost impossible to find any New Zealand hands reaching out to hang on to a Lion, so comprehensive had been the All Black victories, but they did put them together to applaud the unstinting work of Jones, who had arrived as a replacement. I don't suppose the irony was lost on them that on a tour on which no expense had been spared to lay the ground in the most meticulous way possible, only a player not originally selected stood out.

There is a player from long ago I should like to mention: Clem Thomas. It was the Swansea flanker who cross-kicked for Ken Jones to score in the last victory by Wales over the All Blacks, in 1953. This does not qualify as an act of invisibility, but I think Clem had licence to roam since centre Bleddyn Williams, with a torn ligament at the top of his thigh, and wing Gareth Griffiths, with a dislocated shoulder, were incapacitated. Clem was the *Observer*'s rugby correspondent when I was playing and we later worked together on the Sunday paper. I used to chuckle when he grew slightly exercised about foul play in the modern game, reminding him that there were some who remembered R.C.C. Thomas as a purveyor of pain by methods that weren't always so very saintly. He tended to splutter a bit at this point: 'Yes, well, ahem,' he would start.

'Yes, Clem?' I'd nudge.

'Never started anything, you know.'

'Really, Clem?'

'Quite happy to finish it, though, ahem . . .'

Clem Thomas

(Colorsport)

England's Nick Jeavons engulfed by Jeff Squire in 1983.

Jeff Squire fancies his chances against the French at Cardiff in 1982.

(Colorsport)

And the other player I'd like to include is Jeff Squire. He went on the 1977 Lions tour of New Zealand as a replacement from the Newport club and came back a Test player aligned with Pontypool. There would be days in the murkiness of the build-up to professionalism in 1995, when players, like Roger Bidgood and Richard Goodey, would go south from Pontypool to Newport, but I suppose it could be called revenge for letting Squire fall under the recruiting spell of Bobby, Charlie, Pricey and Terry Cobner. Apparently they sold the Pooler to him in shifts.

Jeff had a sort of unathletic gait when moving at walking pace, his feet a bit pigeon-toed and his torso slightly pear-shaped while sloping around. But at full tilt he was a lot quicker than he appeared. He was a number 8 by preference, although moving to the blind side never seemed to worry him, and he was a force on two more Lions tours, in 1980 and 1983, before injury on both brought him home prematurely. He could be a stubborn soul, and was, for instance, a ringleader of a body of resistance in New Zealand in 1983, refusing to swap the mauling game that had served the Lions well in 1980 in South Africa for the rucking game dear to Jim Telfer, the coach of the next tour to New Zealand. Not much good has ever come of such divisions and the tour headed inevitably downhill. Until 2005, the tour of 1983 held the record for failure.

Jeff had already resigned from the Welsh team in 1983, having fallen out with the coaches, John Bevan and Terry Cobner, over issues that seemed pretty petty even at the time. I remember there were a couple of meetings held around that time, to do with a professional circus, to be set up by a David Lord. This was a dozen years before rugby union went officially professional, but the first shots were being fired at the establishment and Jeff was standing on the barricade. This places him firmly in the category not so much of the invisible worker, but the rebel 6. The main point is that Jeff was an outstandingly good player, and I think he could be persuaded that this team would make an enormous pile of money through win bonuses. That might make him put aside his stubborn streak and accept the invitation to join the team on its travels, whatever the style of play.

The guvnor and the squire. Terry Cobner (left) admires Jeff Squire's turn of speed for the Lions against Waikato in 1977. (Colorsport)

BLIND-SIDE WING FORWARD

'His vision knew no bounds.'
Open-side wing forward Martyn Williams
skips past South Africa's Pierre Spies at
Cardiff in 2010.

Chapter 12

7

OPEN-SIDE WING FORWARD

The 6 can go about his business as secretively or rebelliously as he likes, but his role is to smother, to keep a lid on things, to lock the opposition in a dark place. The 7 must be conspicuous and visible, a little ray of sunshine. He is the player to whom the coach hands the high-visibility strip before kick-off and orders him to shine.

I once had the honour of playing alongside Jean-Pierre Rives for the Barbarians in the old days of their Easter tour of Wales. I decided the only thing to do was follow him as best I could, to see where he went. Never have I been led to the right place so often, a dog-walker on the end of one of those extendable leads, being pulled around the park by an irrepressible hound. He was an easy target to see, his great mane of blond hair ever out in front; less easy to follow closely, his short legs whirring, his frame launching itself horizontally into the tackle, his hands subtly toying with the ball.

Ahead of his time, Terry Cobner.

Sam Warburton put in a special set of performances at the 2011 World Cup.

Conspicuous in a less hairy way was Terry Cobner. He was not a horizontal defender, but drew ball-carriers into his embrace and then stole the ball from them. He was immensely strong and was so good at working out the angles that would best help him relieve his victims of the ball that they often scarcely felt possession slip from their grasp. Geoff Wheel used to cause an entire maul to shake and shudder as he tore the ball from its innards, but Cob caused barely a ripple with his one-on-one acts of larceny. He was also more of an impact runner with the ball than a deft link, quite happy to dip his shoulder and bounce defenders out of his path.

He was bald before his time but he was also a player ahead of his time, robust on the ball in the style of Michael Jones or Richie McCaw in New Zealand. I am reluctant to make too many comparisons with New Zealand and their wing forwards, because they think, with some justification, that their 'loosies' are a cut above the rest, and might point out that both Jones and McCaw offer options at the line-out. Jumping was possibly not one of Cob's strong points, but he was a force on the world stage, no question, and he could quite reasonably make the point of his own that he helped shape the Lions pack of 1977, perhaps the most all-consuming ever to have toured New Zealand.

To make an impression in New Zealand in the number 7 position requires a special set of performances. And Sam Warburton in the course of five games and 18 minutes placed himself in line to become the outstanding player, and certainly the most impressive captain, at the 2011 World Cup. And on course for inclusion ahead of all others in this team of ours. But then came his tackle on Vincent Clerc. I refuse to call it a 'spear' tackle, but it was a 'tip' tackle, where he lifted the French winger up in the air and dropped him. According to the guidelines of the time, drawn up with player safety in mind, the referee, Alain Rolland, had no other choice but to dismiss him. My only points would be that one tip tackle is not necessarily like another and that a referee should always be given the flexibility to interpret each case on its demerits. A yellow card would have been appropriate.

The irony was that Wales's captain had done nothing up to that point but offer a completely redrafted version of the Welsh rugby player: without a trace of hysteria, utterly grounded and driven by a ferocious ambition. He said the captaincy did not come naturally to him. If so, he managed to fool the entire rugby world. He looked a complete natural. It was bizarre – and a triumph for that old Welsh

The real McCaw and the young pretender.
New Zealand's World-Cup-winning captain
Richie McCaw shakes hands with Sam Warburton
after their encounter at Cardiff in 2010.

John Taylor, kicker of goals.   (Colorsport)

Cardiff Blues' Martyn Williams kicks for goal during the penalty shoot-out against Leicester Tigers.

feeling that if it can go wrong it will – that he should be the one to be sent off. With a deep sense of regret, I shall have to exclude him from the final team, but if he carries on at this rate he will soon be there. He is going to be very special in his own unconventional way.

More conventional as a link between forwards and backs was John Taylor. It might be said he was a Welsh version of Rives, with a plentiful head of hair, but it would have to be noted that there was no sense of chic about the Taylor version. His beard and mop were not so much Gallic as Basil Brush. He was of his time, the 1960s and 70s.

'He's not playing. The man's a communist,' exclaimed Brigadier Glyn Hughes, the secretary of the Barbarians, when it was suggested Taylor be selected to face the All Blacks in 1973. That was because Taylor had refused, after touring with the Lions in 1968, to have anything more to do with apartheid South Africa, which means he is a member of a small club of players dropped for being principled. His stand also meant he denied himself the chance of adding 1974 to his list of achievements.

Still, top of that list remains a place in all four of the Lions Tests in New Zealand in 1971. He was a tireless supporter of the ball and a gifted intermediary with exceptional handling skills. And of course he could kick, his left boot entering the annals of legend for its conversion of Gerald Davies's late try against Scotland at Murrayfield in 1971. If I hesitate over the automatic inclusion of one of the greats of the Welsh back row it is because on the Lions tour of that same year there was a feeling that the back row needed to be altered, beefed up a bit after the third Test, to counter the New Zealand trio of Ian Kirkpatrick, Alan McNaughton and Alex Wyllie. Taylor was dropped for Fergus Slattery, only to be reinstated when the Irishman fell ill with tonsillitis.

Still, it's not the mishap of being dropped that keeps him out. Back then, he retook his place and was outstanding in the final two Tests. But here he must give way. It's this thing about kicking – and not because John Taylor could and did in 1971, but because Martyn Williams couldn't and didn't for the Cardiff Blues in 2009. It wasn't even in an international match, but during a penalty shoot-out after extra time in a Heineken Cup semi-final against Leicester. And it certainly didn't lead to ridicule being heaped upon his head. But for somebody who wears the Hi-Vis shirt of the open-side and who lives in the spotlight on the field this must have been a terrible moment: the

A black-eyed Martyn Williams steps inside New Zealand's Joe Rokocoko, with Gethin Jenkins and Ryan Jones (right) on hand.

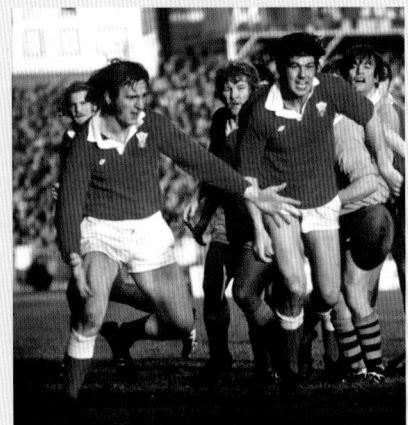
Trevor Evans (left) about to gather loose ball against Australia. (Colorsport)

Paul Ringer (right) leaves the field of play at Twickenham in 1980. (Colorsport)

Steve Hansen, former Wales coach, and New Zealand's World-Cup-winning assistant coach.

hooked place kick in front of the posts, the miss that sent Leicester, not the Blues to the final.

What, a sympathy vote? After all the cruel omissions – without even a mention of Glyn Davidge, Trevor Evans, Paul Ringer, Clive Burgess, Paul Moriarty, Richie Collins or David Pickering – one of the most prestigious positions goes to a bloke who missed a kick? Well, there's a little more to the selection than that, even if it must be acknowledged that throughout his long career of 99 caps, he was never the most fearsome tackler on the planet. It was something Lynn Howells, his coach at Pontypridd in the early days, used to work on; it was an aspect that worried Graham Henry and Steve Hansen when they were coaches of Wales. His defence improved under them all, but it shall be conceded that knocking people over is not the reason for selecting him.

He developed a successful mugging routine for stealing the ball, almost as stealthy as Terry Cobner's, but nor is this why he is selected. Martyn Williams is in because of his love of the finer points of the game. His vision knew no bounds and if not everything he tried could ever have come off he never stopped trying to add a little colour to the canvas. Even if he was doing the simple things, the basics of taking a pass and giving one, the point it made was the exact opposite of the act: this is not as easy as I've just made it look.

It was Steve Hansen who identified the source of the quest to add a little glitter to life as a forward: 'He's a frustrated centre.' A little light on the searing pace required to rule the midfield, he was not tough enough to go into the pack and throw his weight around there. So he built himself his own little theatre, a halfway house between the two worlds and developed a one-man routine that was spellbinding. Everything here was slightly different. Even when he pulled down the curtain on himself he found he was called back on stage for more. He was phoned by the new coach of Wales, Warren Gatland, and returned as the outstanding performer in the 2008 Grand Slam, completing his comeback with the final try against France to seal the clean sweep. As usual, he knew exactly where to be at the right time. He could see things, a pinprick of a hole, the possibility of a pass, a few square centimetres of space, undetected by anyone else. And he had the set of skills that permitted him to thread the whole ball through these fractions. All the skills, that is, except the ability to aim a weary leg at the ball and land the kick that would take the Cardiff Blues to the

Martyn 'Nugget' Williams on his way to clinch the Grand Slam against France in 2008.

'All yours now, son!' Martyn Williams, in Barbarian black and white, hands over the mantle of Welsh openside wing forward to Sam Warburton at Cardiff in June 2011.

Smash and grab. Stephen Jones (10), Leigh Halfpenny and Martyn Williams (right) get to grips with South Africa's Jean De Villiers at Cardiff in 2008.

final of the Heineken Cup. Seeing him stranded in the middle of the Millennium Stadium, running a tired hand through the remains of his ginger hair, merely cemented his special place in the story of rugby in Wales.

It is an indulgence, I admit. But part of the brief to this team must be to send a current of electricity through the crowd. Shane and Gerald and Phil are generators on their own, but Martyn Williams will make the circuit complete.

OPEN-SIDE WING FORWARD

'The best of the very best.'
Number eight Mervyn Davies draws the
Springbok tacklers on the 1974 Lions tour.

(Colorsport)

Chapter 13

8

NUMBER EIGHT

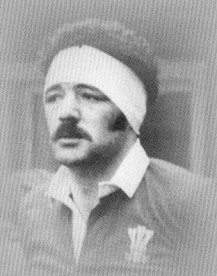

The best is saved until last. Somebody here stands tall. But we must mull over others that have packed down in the middle of the back row, and a special word first for John Gwilliam, captain of two Grand Slams, in 1950 and 1952, a player who has received little credit for the postwar rugby boom in Wales. Gwilliam went on to become headmaster of Birkenhead School and it is said that he is remembered for his disciplinary standards and his religious views. They may have struck an odd note in the changing room, which may help explain why he was dropped four times. Welsh rugby has irreverence for all things.

The Quinnells, for example, were possibly not the best advertisement for the joys of the gym. But they were naturally perfect for their sport. Derek and his sons, Scott and Craig, offered Wales a subterranean centre of gravity and, above the ground, frames that

From the juggernaut school of ball-carrying, Scott Quinnell drives into the Argentinians.

must have set records at the grocers' of Llanelli. Perhaps Phil Davies, who did become a slave to the weights and forced himself up into the category of worthy regent between the reigns of Quinnell I and Quinnell II may have eaten as much, but he was up against an entire family. They were all of the juggernaut school of ball-carrying, with large, supple hands and a general vastness thereafter, every bit of them maintained in an upright position, no matter what they ran into, by some unseen keel beneath their feet. If New Zealand have the Maoris, we have the Quinnells.

Here is a sample of their special moments, all of them funnily enough against France: Derek running through the crowd at the old Arms Park to win his first cap in 1972. Eight Frenchmen were bowled over by Quinnell senior that day, nothing compared with the eighty Welsh back-slappers he scattered to make it on to the field. Scott's try in 1994, after a run so tight against the touchline that it seemed impossible for him to stay in play. That keel did its job. Craig's try in Paris in 1999, a gallop and dive that shook the Stade de France, the thunder behind the lightning of Wales's first win away against the French since 1975.

Large, supple hands and general vastness allow Craig Quinnell to open a hole in the Irish defence.

'Is it safe to come out now?' Scott Quinnell about to deliver the ball to Rupert Moon (9), shielded by (from the left) Emyr Lewis, Garin Jenkins, Phil Davies, Gareth Llewellyn and John Davies.

There is a third son, Gavin, a fourth heavy goods vehicle, who was forced to give up the game after losing an eye following an incident in a club match between Llanelli and Cross Keys. It is a sad statistic in rugby as played nowadays that every fourth player in any squad is unavailable through injury, and not even a family as mighty as the Quinnells is exempt.

Scott is going to bear the family coat of arms at number 8, perhaps because he was the sharpest off the mark from the base of the scrum. He won 52 caps for Wales, which was remarkable given that he suffered from rheumatoid arthritis in his knees and from other assorted ailments. He missed the business end of the victorious 1997 Lions tour to South Africa, for instance, because he had to undergo a hernia operation. Being a Quinnell, it was of course a double hernia. He would also have won more caps if he had not gone to Wigan in rugby league in 1994. He returned to union in 1996, stepping into the new, openly paid world with Richmond. Perhaps he was at his best on the 2001 Lions tour to Australia, gaining those precious yards from number 8 at a time when defences were set not five yards back, but in line with the rear of the scrum.

Running well with the ball was a speciality of Alun Pask, who was positively Fijian in the way he held it in one hand and set off at speed for a point far in the distance. Playing in the Pacific style wasn't necessarily always the chosen manner at Abertillery Park, but never let it be said that the Valleys can't be quirky. Because he is best remembered for the spectacular – there is a celebrated photo of him diving for a try in the corner at Twickenham in 1966 – his defensive work was never so acclaimed, but his pursuit and tackle of Henri Rancoule, the French wing, in 1962 grabbed the attention of the Lions selectors and guaranteed him a place on the tour that summer to South Africa. He played for the Lions again in 1966, and there were many who said that he should have been appointed tour captain, instead of Mike Campbell-Lamerton.

The following year, his brother David died, way before his time, and Alun, at the age of 29, simply called a halt to his rugby. In later years he would re-engage with the game through television at BBC Wales. He used to come in to log the matches as they were being recorded, and over many years his squiggles and stars provided an immaculate record not only of what was happening in Welsh rugby, but also whether it was any good. I remember the terrible day in November 1995 when we heard that he had gone back into his house that was ablaze, and had perished.

Toby Faletau, another success story from the 2011 World Cup.

Mervyn Davies, king of the line-out, seizes control.

And so it is on a sad note that we come to Mervyn Davies. It is not entirely inappropriate, for this is a final chapter with an element of suffering. In late March 1976 the number 8 was playing for Swansea against Pontypool in a cup-tie, when he collapsed with an intra-cranial haemorrhage. Four years earlier, playing for his then club London Welsh against London Irish, he had felt severe pains in his skull, but it had been diagnosed as meningitis. This meant that at the peak of his rugby powers he had a time bomb ticking inside his head.

Merv the Swerve was as tall and pencil-slender as the Quinnells were broad and anchored. He was most certainly not what they call nowadays a maker of the hard yards, although no doubt a conditioner of today would put some muscle on his lankiness. Perhaps it would spoil him, because by way of compensation for not being a wrecking ball, he became a peerless distributor of the rugby ball, mostly in the direction of Gareth Edwards, who could do all the bursting of three men if given a little time and space. Davies was the purveyor of those conditions to his scrum-half, perhaps not as extravagant a passer as Michael Owen in the Grand Slam of 2005, but accurate and always governed by common sense and a knowledge of what was plausible. If he had to take contact he appeared indestructible, picking himself up from collisions his frame did not seem designed to absorb. It is remarkable that this symbol of external physical durability should all the while have been menaced by critical internal meltdown.

His height and slimness were beneficial elsewhere, giving him mobility and an athleticism that, allied to a wonderful appetite for tackling, made him a master of defence. For one so tall and upright he could assume in a flash the low, technically correct position to take down an opponent. He was fearless, too, at throwing himself on the ball. If he had a serious condition looming inside his head, it went alongside the less tangible mental issue of being a nutter. The word is used not to describe someone unable to contain a lust for violent conduct, for in that respect Merv was a self-defender and never an aggressor, but is reserved for a player who was unthinkingly and unbelievably courageous on the field. He played in 38 consecutive Test matches between 1969 and his enforced retirement in 1976, just after he had led Wales to the Grand Slam. He went on two Lions tours, the best that have ever been, in 1971 and 1974. In 46 international appearances for his country and the Lions, he lost only nine times.

Mervyn Davies, the basketball player, manufactures a pass against Scotland.

Michael Owen, an extravagant passer, and captain of the 2005 Grand Slam side.

Mervyn Davies, proving a handful for South Africa in 1974. (Colorsport)

Most important, his height and lightness made him king of the line-out. Even in these days of the assisted leap, it is all-important to have the ability to take to the air quickly. Merv rose unaided and dominated the tail, where the best ball is won, opening up the heart of the midfield to immediate attack. I suspect that I have overused the Lions tour of 1971 as a reference point, but I am going back there one last time, back to the only successful tour of New Zealand, back to the judgement of the greatest All Black forward of all time, Sir Colin 'Pine Tree' Meads. 'The one player who stopped us beating the Lions in 1971,' he told me, 'was Mervyn Davies. We loved peeling round the tail of the line-out, and aim at a weak point of the defence. We had Barry John all lined up. Once we were rumbling that way, we reckoned we were pretty unstoppable. But Mervyn beat us at the back. He was the one that won the series.'

Since the end of his playing days, Mervyn has cut something of a lugubrious figure. In his autobiography, In Strength and Shadow, he says he hit a low point in the early days of his life without rugby, depressed, drinking too much. Even now he may be not the first port of call for anyone in search of a chuckle. I don't know whether this might offer him an opportunity to smile, but he goes into this team not only as the best number 8, but also the best of the very best, the outstanding player in a selection of stars. I would hand the captaincy to Phil Bennett and let Bobby Windsor sort out the pack and tell Merv the Swerv to go out there and simply enjoy himself.

Chapter 14

THE GREATEST WELSH XV EVER

15	J.P.R. WILLIAMS
14	GERALD DAVIES
13	BLEDDYN WILLIAMS
12	JAMIE ROBERTS
11	SHANE WILLIAMS
10	PHIL BENNETT (capt.)
9	GARETH EDWARDS
1	GETHIN JENKINS
2	BOBBY WINDSOR
3	GRAHAM PRICE
4	R.H. WILLIAMS
5	ROBERT NORSTER
6	JEFF SQUIRE
7	MARTYN WILLIAMS
8	MERVYN DAVIES